THE GARDEN AT BUCKINGHAM PALACE

An Illustrated History

THE GARDEN AT BUCKINGHAM PALACE

An Illustrated History

JANE BROWN

PHOTOGRAPHS BY
CHRISTOPHER SIMON SYKES

ROYAL COLLECTION PUBLICATIONS

Published by
Royal Collection Enterprises Ltd
St James's Palace, London SW1A 1JR

For a complete catalogue of current publications, please write to the
address above, or visit our website on www.royal.gov.uk

© 2004 Royal Collection Enterprises Ltd
Text by Jane Brown, photographs by Christopher Simon Sykes,
and reproductions of all items in the Royal Collection
© 2004 HM Queen Elizabeth II.

128454

ISBN 1 902163 82 6

British Library Cataloguing in Publication Data:
A catalogue record for this book is available from the British Library.

Designed by Karen Stafford
Produced by Book Production Consultants plc, Cambridge
Printed and bound by ContiTipocolor, Italy

FRONT COVER: The herbaceous border in high summer.

PAGE 1: Autumn: looking down towards the west front of the Palace.
Buddleja forrestii in the foreground, with *Azara lanceolata* (whose flowers
smell of chocolate) behind.

PAGES 2 AND 3: Adriaen van Diest, *Buckingham House and garden from
Constitution Hill*, *c.*1703 (detail, see page 36).

PAGE 6: The herbaceous border in early summer. The archway marks
The Queen's entrance from the forecourt of the Palace. The plants
include phlox, red-hot pokers, and the yellow *Inula magnifica*, which can
grow up to 2½ metres (8 feet) in a year. Ornamental grasses, swaying
in the breeeze, provide an almost ghostly filigree above the other
plants.

BACK COVER: Laurits Regner Tuxen (1853–1927), *Queen Victoria's
Diamond Jubilee Garden Party, 28 June 1897*, oil on canvas, 1897–1900.

PAGES 208–9: Early narcissi and crocuses, with one of the
garden's magnolias just coming into bloom. This area was the
Victorian 'Round Bed', and later in the year is full of
bluebells and fritillaries.

PAGE 210: Looking from the island in mid-winter.

PAGE 212: *Magnolia x soulangeana* 'Amabilis'.

PAGE 215: *Magnolia* 'Vulcan', one of the darkest of the
magnolias, which flowers from an early age.

PAGE 216: The west front of the Palace from the island in
autumn.

PAGE 220: Pheasant's eye narcissi surround the trunk of a
dead tree – left by the gardeners as a woodpecker nests there
annually.

PAGE 224: The path from the so-called 'Electrician's Gate':
behind the back of the Mound, with the Mews on the right,
and into one of the most famous gardens in the world.

ENDPAPERS: The garden in the 1880s; and the garden today,
after a fall of snow.

Contents

Gardens may have been in certain places for many years, but, unlike old buildings, they are in a constant state of change. The development of the garden at Buckingham Palace reflects the interests of the occupants of the house and talents of its Head Gardeners, but it also has a life of its own. Apart from regular invasions by guests to the annual Garden Parties, and the occasional visits by helicopters, it remains a virtual natural oasis in the middle of a bustling capital city.

The history of the garden is well documented, but this book has the added attraction of some really splendid illustrations, which, together with the informative text, conveys the very special character of the garden and of both its populations of domestic plants and natural inhabitants. I am sure that it will be much appreciated by all who delight in gardens.

INTRODUCTION

The lawn and west front of the Palace in late autumn. The two bronze cranes, visible under the tree to the right, were presented to King Edward VII during a visit to India as Prince of Wales in 1875–6. The curiously 'bonsai'-shaped Chinese chestnut is, perhaps (after the 1987 hurricane), the largest specimen in the country.

LONDON SEEMS to make a speciality of newly washed mornings so dazzlingly bright that every outline shimmers; 'Queen's Weather' they called it in the late nineteenth century. On such mornings now, in spring and early summer, the crowd around the Victoria Memorial – sitting on the steps, swinging their legs from the balustrades, strolling, clicking their cameras, just watching – are players on a stage that has changed little in ninety years. The Palace forecourt's gold-tipped railings glitter in the sunshine, the red tulips in The Queen's Gardens blaze in harmony with the tunics of her Guards, the Royal Standard flutters from the flagpole, the gates open and close as the daily business at one of the most famous addresses in the world follows its unruffled course. This morning melts into all those other mornings; only the clothes and camera technology separate this crowd from when 'Christopher Robin went down with Alice' to watch the Changing of the Guard, or from Virginia Woolf's evocation of such a morning in *Mrs Dalloway*, capturing its significance in eleven words – 'It was June. The King and Queen were at the Palace.'[1]

This famous, almost iconic image of the east front – the Grand Entrance to the Sovereign's official London residence – presides over our collective memory of national griefs and celebrations: the long façade with rows of tall windows and a stern paternal stare has a stolidity that is partly architectural and partly constitutional, earned by standing firm through turbulent decades. This is the newest part of the Palace, the east wing designed by Edward Blore and built by Thomas Cubitt for Queen Victoria and Prince Albert in 1847, but the original Caen stone proved so unsatisfactory that the front had to be refaced in Portland stone, under Aston Webb's supervision, as the completion of the Victoria Memorial scheme in 1913.

In contrast, the western façade on the garden side is less familiar: it sprawls rather somnolently, John Nash's ornamented but serene west front for George IV, in biscuit-coloured Bath stone which glows in the afternoon sun. Nash's Bow Room opens onto the broad terrace with steps down to the lawn, the setting for The Queen's garden parties, but also having the distinction of being the oldest helicopter pad in London, in use for fifty years. Beyond the lawn the garden dissolves into tree-shaded groves and paths around and beyond the lake, which – in the absence of the helicopter – preserve an almost uncanny sense of mystery and calm. In common with all London gardens, this garden is overlooked by tall buildings, and has been since the Palace Hotel in Buckingham Gate was built in the 1840s. For the price of a bus ticket from Hyde Park Corner to Victoria a glimpse of the garden has long been included. Somehow the mystery survives.

Even – perhaps especially – on the big occasions, this secret garden retreats behind the willow fronds. When the lawn is crowded with the July garden-party visitors, even when those camera lenses and thousands of pairs of eyes gazed intently upon the star-studded stages for the 2002 Golden Jubilee concerts, the garden entertains, then regains its green quiet. At the second, the

'pop' concert, did The Queen, more familiar with her garden than anyone else, smile knowingly as Sir Barry Humphries quipped, as one garden-owner to another, that she must not worry about the lawn?

This garden is a remarkable place: it is an ecological rarity as an isolated habitat of some 16 hectares (39 acres) walled for 150 years in the centre of a great city; it is socially pre-eminent because it is The Queen's garden and within it certain traditions are respected. It has always been a private garden, though adjacent to the royal parks to which people have had access since the seventeenth century. The garden, no less than the Palace, would seem to possess a symbolism that adorns the uniqueness of the British Crown.

In the following pages the garden takes centre stage, and the Palace is regarded rather as some giant's casket of treasures set down in the garden. For architectural and art history the Palace is well served by John Martin Robinson's *Buckingham Palace: the Official Illustrated History* (2000), and for a fuller social history by Edna Healey's *The Queen's House*, published in 1997. There has been a book about the garden before, the highly entertaining but now sadly rare *The Gardens of Buckingham Palace* by Peter Coats, published in 1978; he was a member of the cotton-spinning family, a soldier and former viceregal aide-de-camp, who became a garden designer and garden editor of *House & Garden* magazine. In his foreword to that book The Duke of Edinburgh called it 'this history and detailed anatomy of this piece of land and all its plant and animal residents and visitors'. That was in the light of the first natural history surveys, made in the 1960s; the ongoing recording and surveys of the 1990s by members of the London Natural History Society similarly inform this book, especially

Chapter 4. Further use was made of the garden's natural history by Dr David Bellamy in *The Queen's Hidden Garden: Buckingham Palace's Treasury of Wild Plants*, with botanical drawings by Marjorie Lyon (1984), also referred to in Chapter 4.

Royal gardens collectively have received much attention, but as there is such an enormously rich history, from medieval hunting parks via Tudor extravaganzas and William III and Queen Mary's Hampton Court to the delights of Richmond and Kew, there is usually little space left for a mid-eighteenth-century latecomer like Buckingham Palace. More importantly, these earlier royal gardens can be visited at almost any time and they have been frequently filmed and photographed. The photographs in this book, taken through the seasons by Christopher Simon Sykes, are the first such revelation of the garden of Buckingham Palace.

Prince Philip's phrase 'anatomy of this piece of land' is reminiscent of the words 'this favourite spot of Ground', which open Chapter 1 and which come from the 1763 deed of purchase of the Duke of Buckingham's house by George III.[2] The 'favourite spot' came into being simply by being left outside the pale of Henry VIII's hunting park of St James's: a place where the poachers escaped, where Elizabethan drovers leaned over the fence, resting before their last stretch to the Horseferry, where James I set up his mulberry-growing enterprise, and where the Cromwellian soldiers were billeted in Cavalier Lord Goring's new house and garden.

An accident of design history led to the creation of the site for Buckingham Palace, when in the euphoria of his Restoration Charles II had St James's Park redesigned in the formal French manner beloved of his mother, Queen Henrietta Maria, a great gardener. The design device, a *patte d'oie* or goose-foot, was of avenues and vistas radiating from Whitehall, with The Mall avenue ending at

The west front of the Palace at evening, showing the terrace, the Bow Room entrance to the garden, and one of Nash's flanking conservatories.

what was then Lord Arlington's house. Whether there was anything more than geometry behind this finger of fate remains supposition, but the symbolism, so much a part of seventeenth-century gardens, is worth noting. The design from Catholic France, implemented by a French royal gardener, must have been appreciated by Lord Arlington (who made a Catholic's death) and was to be utilised by his successor, the Duke of Buckingham, who also died a Catholic. In the more secular world after the Hanoverian succession, the crowds of Georgian court beauties and their beaux who thronged The Mall were halted at the Duke's gates. Any religious symbolism had been forgotten; the value of the Duke of Buckingham's house lay in its beautiful, fashionably formal and private garden.

It was George II's Queen, Caroline of Ansbach, who was so irked by the crowds around St James's Palace that she asked Prime Minister Robert Walpole what it would cost to regain the Park as a private garden. Walpole's artful reply, 'Only three CROWNS, madame'[3] – a crown was then a coin worth about 5 shillings – was not wasted on the politically wise Queen. So her son, Frederick, Prince of Wales, set his sights upon Buckingham House and its peaceful garden after the Duke's death in 1721. The Prince was a keen gardener and he remembered the nightingales that sang in a little wilderness there, but the widowed Duchess would not sell. Sadly, in 1751 Frederick succumbed to

In recent years a winter fall of snow has become a rarity in most gardens in the south-east of England. Here an unexpected snowfall gives the lawn and west front of the Palace an unusually Russian air.

Augustin Heckel (c.1690–1770),
A view from Constitution Hill to West Minster,
pencil and watercolour, 1734. RCIN 917612

A View from Constitution Hill towards West Minster 1734. Al.

James Duffield Harding (1798–1863),
The Crystal Palace, watercolour, 1854 (detail).
Harding was a child prodigy, and a prolific
watercolourist and illustrator. His view of
the gardens of the Crystal Palace exhibited
at the Royal Academy in 1854 gives them
the radiance of the Elysian Fields.

pneumonia as the result of being caught in a storm supervising his garden at Kew.[4] His son, who came to the throne as George III in 1760, finally bought the desirable garden and house as a retreat for his wife Charlotte of Mecklenburg-Strelitz and himself.

The privacy of the garden was thus dearly prized and not lightly surrendered, not even when Queen Charlotte used her town house for presentations and entertaining, keeping up appearances when her dear but increasingly afflicted husband was confined at Windsor Castle. Somewhat perversely, in the world of gardening priorities, this also meant that the garden was never given over entirely to a great 'name' designer: John Evelyn, Henry Wise, 'Capability' Brown and William Chambers have all entered the story by now, yet none of them would be able to call this garden their creation. This theme of 'Precious Privacy' – the right of every subject in their garden – is followed through eight reigns in Chapter 2. History is hedged with the usual constraints of money and time, the first operated by the Treasury's control over a constitutional monarchy, the second the prerogative of an even higher authority. George III had bought Buckingham House for £28,000; additional money was spent on the house for Queen Charlotte but almost nothing on the garden, where the crisp formalism that the Duke of Buckingham left behind was gradually softened and blurred by nature. George III's Britain had expensive wars with America and France to pay for, and by the time Napoleon had been defeated at Waterloo in 1815 the King was in no fit state to go garden-making; Queen Charlotte, ever a contented soul, was happy in her prettily picturesque and favourite garden at Frogmore.

The tranquil, parkland atmosphere of the garden is its outstanding characteristic for the visitor. Two of the garden's plane trees, and an oak, in the area occupied in the Victorian garden by the 'Round Bed'.

Even as Regent for his father, George IV would never have turned his mother out of her house, but she died in 1818, followed by George III in 1820. George IV chose and named 'Buckingham Palace' as his principal residence and spent lavishly on the building, as he had on his previous architectural passions of Royal Lodge, Brighton Pavilion and Carlton House. But George IV had waited so long for his throne that he had little time left for the garden. William IV had even less time, a reign of seven years, 1830–37, and he disliked Buckingham Palace, offering it as a replacement for the Houses of Parliament when they were destroyed by fire in 1834. Parliament declined his offer.

Making a garden does take more time than merely building – as Francis Bacon had prophesied at the end of the sixteenth century: 'when ages grow to civility and elegancy, men come to build stately sooner than to garden finely; as if gardening were the greater perfection'.[5] A more modern source, the architect and landscape architect Sir Geoffrey Jellicoe (1900–1996), always asserted that 'the laggard' garden design 'of all the arts none takes so long to come to maturity, and none is so liable to deterioration and destruction'.[6] If the priorities of the building costs and two short reigns had failed to secure a grand design for Buckingham Palace, a long reign would surely provide the visionary space? Monogrammed flower beds, gravelled vistas and fountains, statues and pavilions – these were all essential adornments to the many great gardens of Britain and so must surely be right for a palace?

Such a garden was to be made in Victorian England, but for the Crystal Palace when it was re-erected on its permanent site at Sydenham. The Queen opened the garden in 1854. At home Queen Victoria gave Prince Albert – who felt himself a natural gardener – charge of all her estate and garden matters and he made immediate improvements at Buckingham Palace. He master-minded an exquisitely decorated pavilion as a retreat for the Queen, undoubtedly the most innovative project so far, but his attentions were diverted to his new house and garden at Osborne on the Isle of Wight, to the Great Exhibition and then Balmoral Castle. And then he was gone: Albert's too-early death in 1861 almost certainly deprived Buckingham Palace of a 'Victorian' garden – it removed his progressive spur to many arts and sciences – and his grieving widow neglected her Palace for years on end. The bywords of Queen Victoria's 64-year reign became 'No <u>changes</u>, no <u>changes</u>',[7] though there were some lighter moments, as these pages will show.

King Edward VII succeeded his mother for a brief nine years, 1901–10; they were glorious years, and the King enjoyed his country garden in the city. His son, King George V, inherited a throne and 'the war to end all wars', 1914–18, which broke the heart of England as a country where great gardens were made, and left many to decay and dereliction.

At Buckingham Palace the almost inhuman requirements of an hereditary crown cast their shadows over the garden's story. The workload of a modern monarchy, as of King George V and Queen Mary in the 1920s, left little time for light-hearted interests. Their subjects, notably the enormously energetic merchant banker Lionel de Rothschild at Exbury in Hampshire and Major Lawrence Johnston at Hidcote Manor in Gloucestershire, might be planting large flower gardens, but no such flamboyance could be allowed at the Palace. The time for garden-making here was past; from now on it would be rather more of a confirmation of gardening virtues, of the careful management of plants in their setting. The paradoxes loom; whilst there was the sensibility that kept the memory of a non-royal duke in the Palace's name, that sense of continuity that marks a Chatsworth or a Castle Howard as the beating heart of a great estate seemed to evaporate in London. Whilst stately homes may restore their historic garden features, the recall of the Duke of Buckingham's great formal garden is clearly out of the question here. Sadly, Queen Victoria's painted Pavilion, one of the most enchanting innovations in the garden, was demolished in 1928, at a time when an appreciation of historic garden buildings was but a dream.

Canada geese, among the garden's most frequent and numerous visitors, gather to feed beneath one of the bronze cranes by the lake.

The vagaries of the management of the garden aggravated this situation: in 1851 Prince Albert had brought the garden under the control of the Lord Steward's department of the Royal Household, but in 1901 it was taken 'out' again, to the Office of Works, which devolved down the century into the Ministry of Works, then into the Department of the Environment. The endemic changes of governments, departmental heads and personnel further fragmented a situation to which a garden is far more susceptible than a building, and which can only be ameliorated by long-serving head gardeners, as Chapter 4 will show. Since 1992 the garden has been the responsibility of the Royal Household, in the department of the Keeper of the Privy Purse, The Queen's Treasurer.

If governmental changes frustrated any long-term planning on the garden, there were further complications in the drastic upheavals at the end of each reign. The obligatory moving out and moving in at times of the greatest stress and emotion punctuate this story with sadness. The nadir was 1936, 'the year of three kings' – the broken-hearted Queen Mary had to move out, and her eldest son, King Edward VIII, was loath to move in. After months of tensions and rumours King Edward abdicated, and King George VI and Queen Elizabeth were cata-

Looking across to the Bow Room and Music Room. The island in the lake is on the left.

pulted into positions they had neither expected nor wanted. Was it then that the unchangeableness of the garden, where the steady ritual of the seasons reigned, became most appreciated?

Prince Albert had invented the art of gardening elsewhere, at Osborne where all the royal children had their own gardens; King George VI and Queen Elizabeth, who both loved gardening, perfected it as far as they were able, at Windsor and Sandringham. A most telling detail is that in her widowhood Queen Elizabeth The Queen Mother found solace in her gardens at Royal Lodge, Birkhall and the Castle of Mey.

If Buckingham Palace was ever going to have a great formal garden, it would have been on the ceremonial east front. Chapters 1 and 3 trace the long entanglements of history between St James's Park and the Palace and the evolution of the Victoria Memorial as one of the most emotive gathering grounds in the world.

The very public status of the 'front garden' only serves to enhance the serenity of the lawns and groves beyond the west face of the Palace, to where relatively few people go and then only by invitation. This 'back garden' has become a unique and fascinating wildlife sanctuary, providing habitats for entomological curiosities, for birds rarely seen in London (common sandpiper, sedge warbler and lesser whitethroat), with smew and goosander on the lake in winter; and for trees (the very rare Chinese chestnut *Castanea mollissima*, the lily-of-the-valley tree *Clethra arborea*) and many other shrubs and flowers, all in a diversity that has been purposefully widened in the last forty years.[8] Chapter 4 reveals how this very important garden has managed to become a pioneer in rich-habitat gardening.

A garden is the ultimate celebration of a place: the final chapter traces some of the history of the garden parties and celebrations that have been held here. The annual garden parties and the summer openings of the Palace now present the most widely seen images of the garden, but more than four hundred years of history on 'this favourite spot of Ground' have contrived an integrity of place, a tranquillity, that is not easily disturbed. It remains, essentially, a serene and enchanted garden – The Queen's garden.

I

'... *this favourite
spot of Ground ...*'

THE QUEEN'S PALACE AND RICHMOND,
INDENTURE DATED 20 APRIL 1763

I

AN ACCIDENT OF DESIGN
Henry VIII to William IV

The west front of Buckingham Palace, photographed from the Mound on a snowy winter morning. The core of the original 17th-century Buckingham House is still enclosed within the central block of the present-day Palace.

SURVEYORS AND LAWYERS are all too often the chief influences on a garden's history, and Buckingham Palace is no exception. In the Royal Library at Windsor is a slim, red-morocco-bound volume, carefully hand-scripted and illustrated with watercoloured plans, of lawyerly 'Extracts' from the records in the Surveyor General's Office 'relating to the Freehold and Leasehold Estates purchased By His Majesty of Sir Charles Sheffield … now called the Queen's Palace'. The indenture or conveyance was dated 20 April 1763, a contract made between the Duke of Buckingham's heir, Sir Charles Sheffield, and John, Earl of Bute, and Philip Carteret Webb, acting as trustees for George III.[1] The price was £28,000. The King had bought it for his wife, his young Queen, the former Princess Sophie Charlotte of Mecklenburg-Strelitz, whom he had married on 8 September 1761; he prided himself on his Britishness, and in a nod to the old royal residence of Greenwich, and Inigo Jones's exquisite Queen's House – used by the Stuart queens Anne of Denmark and Henrietta Maria – this too was to be called 'the Queen's House'. George III and Queen Charlotte's eldest child, George (later the Prince Regent and George IV), was born at St James's Palace on 12 August 1762, but twelve of their later fourteen children were born in the Queen's House, which was their retreat and family home.

The garden's story, like the legal preliminaries to this conveyance, goes back well over two hundred years, to the time of Henry VIII. In 1531, tiring of the wrangling over his divorce, Henry had dismissed his Queen, Catherine of Aragon, and was living openly with his new love, Anne Boleyn; they were secretly married in January 1533.[2] In his euphoria Henry had started on a new project referred to as 'the King's whole palace of Westminster', whereby he and Queen Anne would be able to ride freely and privately from Whitehall to Kensington. He acquired the land in the meadows west of Whitehall belonging to the former leper hospital of St James (which Henry VI had given to Eton College in 1449), pensioning off the poor women who lived there.[3] He built a new royal residence there, with gatehouse and chapel, to serve as a hunting lodge (parts survive in the present St James's Palace), and enclosed his deer park, St James's Park, which extended westwards over the hill (across Green Park, then called Upper St James's Park) to the present Hyde Park Corner. He also duly displaced the Benedictine monks from their land in the Manor of Hyde, enclosing the present Hyde Park and Kensington Gardens. The public road from Knightsbridge to Piccadilly, already a main route into London from the west, formed the boundaries of the hunting parks; the road to Westminster branched off southwards at Hyde Park Corner, sweeping in a curve along the west boundary of St James's Park, until it divided, eastwards via Tothill Street to Westminster, and westwards via 'the King's Road' to Chelsea. The fields immediately west of this road were marshy meadows and pastures, crossed by the Tybourne stream as it flowed from its source near the present Marble Arch to the Thames.

The royal surveyors had actually acquired much of this marshy land, part of the old Saxon manor of Eia, which had been divided at the time of the Domesday Book into three smaller manors: Hyde in the north; Ebury (sometimes Eabury or Eybury), which stretched from Hyde Park Corner to the Thames; and Neyte or Neate, the riverside area of Pimlico.[4] Elizabeth I granted most of the area excluded from the hunting parks to Sir Thomas Knyvett on a lease which lasted until 1675[5] – all, that is, except for a plot immediately opposite the west gate of Lower St James's Park. This plot, roughly 125 × 140 yards (115 × 130 metres) – comparable to a traditional walled kitchen garden or a generously sized football pitch – comes into focus as a garden in the reign of Elizabeth's successor, James I, as the site for a project to grow mulberries for the rearing of silkworms.

The 'King's Mulberry Men' were William Stallenge and his nephew Jasper, and they went to great expense and effort during the first two decades of the seventeenth century to wall and cultivate the plot, planting thousands of seedlings of *Morus nigra*, the black mulberry, in rows in four rectangular beds as in a physic garden. The black mulberry was already a garden favourite, having been grown in England for about a hundred years, yielding deliciously juicy dark red fruit and assuming a gnarled and curious form as it aged. It was James I's intention to encourage a silk industry on a par with that of the French, but no one seems to have realised that silkworms prefer to feed on the white mulberry, *Morus alba*, and the project was never a success. But the 'King's Mulberry Men' gained pensions for life, and the name 'The Mulberry Garden' passed into popular legend; stories of surviving mulberries persisted into the early twentieth century, but as so much of the original garden had been built over these too are part of the mythology.

The Mulberry Garden, with its house, was already a desirable residence when Charles I granted it to Lord Aston in 1628; seven years' later, when his lordship took up his appointment as Ambassador to Spain, the silkworm project was finally abandoned.[6] In 1640 Lord Aston's son sold his interest in the Mulberry Garden for £1,000 to Lord Goring, a seasoned courtier and staunch royalist who was Vice-Chamberlain and Master of the Horse in the household of the 'Rose and Lily Queen', Henrietta Maria. Goring already owned a substantial brick and timber house with four gables on land immediately south of the Mulberry Garden: this house, Goring House, faced southwards onto an entrance court 'with a faire paire of gates and paved walke'.[7] At each side of the house there were fashionable formal garden features – a fountain garden, a terrace, a mound or 'mount' (large

Alexander Marshal (*c*.1620–82), *Morus nigra* 'the blak mulburie' from folio 140 of Marshal's *Florilegium*, (RL 24407). The *Florilegium* is the only surviving example of a flower book painted by an English artist in the 17th century. The page also shows a field spaniel, common or grey partridge, the north-west European grass snake (*Natrix natrix*) and blue pimpernel.

Early morning mist and another fall of snow.

enough to have trees planted on the slopes and on the top), and green, shady arbours or tunnels of pleached limes or willows. To the south-west, alongside the road to Chelsea, Goring had his fruit orchard and kitchen garden. He had expanded northwards and westwards into what became known as the Goring Great Garden, a 20-acre (8-hectare) field shaped in the manner of an inebriated hexagon, part of the Lower Crowfields, which he purchased from Sir Thomas Knyvett's successors. Lord Goring was the first to practise a gardener's imagination on this ground; the Mulberry Garden (though only leasehold) completed his compact territory, something over 27 acres (11 hectares) in all, which gave his name to posterity as the assembler of the major part of the site of the future Buckingham Palace.

Time was to run out on Lord Goring's gardening ambitions; his Great Garden was being walled but was little more than a flowery meadow when the Royalists and Parliamentarians began to marshal their forces for civil war. Lord Goring gave his fortune and all but his life in the King's cause, and when defeat came he was imprisoned and then exiled to France. At the Restoration in 1660 he was an elderly man and, though he died in his bed, and in England, aged 80 in 1663, he never regained his Goring House properties. During the Commonwealth period the building had housed the French Ambassador and his retinue, and afterwards officers of the New Model Army, who had ordered defensive fortifications to be built in the Great Garden. By July 1660 the house had been spruced up and Samuel Pepys (1633–1703) took his wife there to 'a great wedding of Nan Hartlib to Mein Herr Roder, which was kept at Goring House with very great estate, cost and noble company'.[8]

The Parliamentary Commissioners, in their itemised reports on the confiscated Royalist properties, provide the most detailed evidence of the gardens they often destroyed or left to decay. At the very time, in the spring of 1642, that Lord Goring was escorting Queen Henrietta Maria to the safety of her old home in France, the Queen's favourite French garden designer, André Mollet (d. *c*.1665), was working on the Queen's last and most fashionable garden at Wimbledon House.

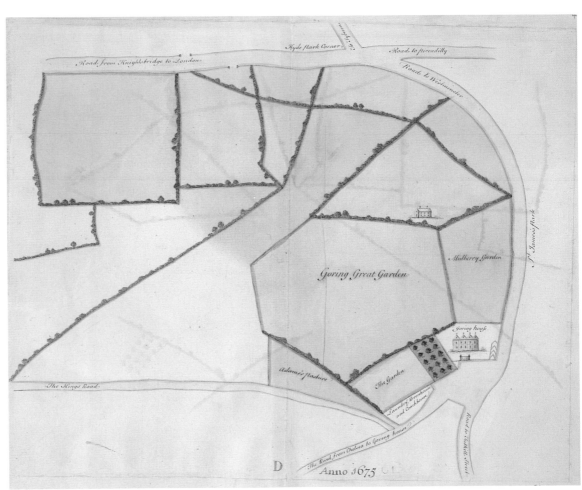

PREVIOUS PAGE Planting in the garden is designed to show it at its best for two particular periods of the year: early spring, when The Queen is in residence, is the first.

ABOVE AND RIGHT Snowdrops and other early spring bulbs have naturalised and spread across the garden, as have broad swathes of jonquils, daffodils and narcissi. The best display of spring bulbs is found in the area previously occupied by, and still referred to as, 'the Kennels'. The two plane trees visible (right) on either side of the police sentry box were planted by Queen Victoria and Prince Albert, and are always the last in the garden to lose their leaves.

ABOVE A show of narcissi in the Rose Garden. The planter was presented to Her Majesty The Queen to mark the Golden Jubilee in 2002.

LEFT The garden is also rich in spring-flowering trees, including many examples of magnolias, which are succeeded by azaleas and rhododendrons.

OVERLEAF The waterfall was installed in the 1990s. The two trees in the foreground are, on the left, a Kentukea, 'Perkin's Pink', and on the right *Magnolia x soulangeana* 'Amabilis'.

On that dangerous journey did the Queen and her brave escort distil the tensions by discussing gardening? The loyal Goring must have been enthused by the Queen's passion for her gardens; both Wimbledon House and Goring House were reported on by the Commissioners in 1651/2, and perhaps the Queen's tastes throw some light on Lord Goring's intentions.

He must have started alterations in the Mulberry Garden, for the Commissioners found a bowling green, an absolute necessity for all gardens of pretension, and also that 'parte thereof is Meanelye planted with several sorts of fruite Trees and the other parte thereof planted with white thorne in the manner of a wildernesse or Maze walkes'.[9] Was this embryonic and undoubtedly neglected maze utilising some of the mulberry plantation, with additional new plants to imitate the new maze at Wimbledon House, where 'wood and sprayes of a good growth and height [were] cutt out into severall meanders', with circles, semi-circles and 'intricate turnings'?[10] Like all gardeners with new ground to fill, Lord Goring must have planned his Great Garden endlessly in his mind: at Wimbledon he knew there was the Orange Garden, divided into four plats or knots 'fitted for the groweth of choyse flowers; bordered with boxs in the poynts, angles, squares and roundles and handsomely turfed in the Intervalls or little walkes thereof'.[11] There were also the Queen's favourite *plats de broderie* to emulate, the groundwork in embroidery that even the Commissioners appreciated, using hyacinths, anemones, jonquils and ranunculus in spring-time.[12] Did his lordship in exile dream of fountains? Goring House garden had a fountain, perhaps in the style of Francesco Fanelli's 'Arethusa' – then in the Queen's garden at Somerset House, surviving now, and much altered, as the Diana Fountain in Bushy Park.

As gardening is an imitative art, some evidence of what Lord Goring had done, or intended to do, may be seen in his neighbour's garden, the Earl of Arundel's Tart Hall, on the opposite corner of the road to Chelsea. The topographical artist Wenceslaus Hollar (1607–77), a refugee from Bohemia, was living at Tart Hall under Arundel's patronage when the Civil War started; Hollar portrayed the young Catherine Howard, an Arundel granddaughter, against a detailed backdrop of the Hall and its gardens. The elegantly gated entrance court is half-hidden behind her skirt, but the large walled flower garden, with a raised terrace on the west and south sides, can be seen clearly. Hollar also gives an impression of the spacious rural setting shared by Goring House and Tart Hall at this time.

Gardens were shattered, as were lives and fortunes, in those 'fantastick' times of civil wars and Puritan rule: Charles I and Henrietta Maria had used their gardens for theatricals with serious meanings, as the metaphor for their belief in the Divine Right of Kings and their rule 'as heaven come down momentarily to earth'.[13] Out of that distant trauma of regicide and revolution came, as a pernicious creeping weed, a native distrust of the expression of power in great formal gardens.

Lord Goring proved to have been all too truly 'cavalier' in his property dealings, and though all the misdeeds of the Interregnum were

Wenceslaus Hollar (1607–77), *Spring*, 1643. Tart Hall and its gardens in the background of an engraving showing Catherine Howard, granddaughter of Hollar's patron, Thomas Howard, 2nd Earl of Arundel. In the right-hand corner a coach emerges from the road to Chelsea, between the walls of Lord Goring's garden and Tart Hall. RCIN 802403

Welcom sweet Lady you doe bring Spring That makes ye Earth to looke so greene
Rich presents of a hopefull Spring   As when see first began to teeme:
                          Spring

cancelled on Charles II's Restoration, there was a chaos of claim and counter-claim. Goring House and the Great Garden, the first mortgaged, the second apparently never paid for in full, reverted to the Manor of Ebury, now in the hands of Hugh Audley, 'the most formidable property lawyer in London'.[14] The Mulberry Garden had been let, and turned into a pleasure garden, when all other such gardens had been closed down. 'My Lady Gerrard treated us at Mulberry Gardens,' wrote John Evelyn in his diary for 10 May 1654, 'now the only place of refreshment about the Town for persons of the best quality to be exceedingly cheeked at.'[15] This rakish popularity continued throughout the 1660s, and was at some time managed by a Mr Chipp, who made alcoves or bays for courting or plotting. Pepys found it 'a wilderness that is somewhat pretty but rude', and a 'silly place', full of 'rascally, whoring sort of people' in the spring of 1668.[16] The Restoration dramatist, Sir Charles Sedley (*c*.1639–1701), called his popular comedy of that year (based on Molière's *L'Ecole des maris*) *The Mulberry Garden*.

Hugh Audley (for whom Audley Street off Park Lane is named) died in 1663, leaving his considerable properties to his nephew Alexander Davies. Davies was struck down in the plague year, 1665, leaving everything to his infant daughter Mary. He also left debts that had to be settled and to pay these Goring House and the Great Garden, now clearly identified as an aspirational

property, were first let and eventually sold to Henry Bennet, Earl of Arlington. (Young Mary Davies, a romantic figure in the history of London, eventually married Thomas Grosvenor, her dowry contributing to the fortunes of the dukes of Westminster, who still own the Grosvenor Estate and are neighbours to Buckingham Palace.)

Lord Arlington was a grandee, wearing as his badge of loyalty a curious black-patched scar on his nose. It had been earned in a Civil War skirmish, before he joined the King in exile. At Charles II's Restoration he became the Secretary of State (and from 1674, Lord Chamberlain), acknowledged as the 'best bred' of the men around the King, apparently able to manage both the royal temper and the royal mistresses. He had a rich Dutch wife, Isabella, and a daughter whom John Evelyn thought 'a sweete child if ever there was any', also called Isabella. She was betrothed when she was 5 to the King's son by Barbara Castlemaine, the 9-year-old Henry Fitzroy, created Duke of Grafton; they were married when Isabella was 12.

Lord Arlington was not a gardener, but a fine garden was a matter of pride to him, both in London and at his country estate, Euston Hall in Suffolk. Most importantly in this story, he had the friendship of that indefatigable gardening authority, founding Fellow of the Royal Society and silviculturist, John Evelyn (1620–1706).

Immediately upon his return to London, Charles II had brought back his mother's favourite gardener André Mollet to restore his garden at St James's Palace. The formal design used was the *patte d'oie*, inspired by Mollet's *Le jardin de plaisir* of 1651. An army of men was set to work to transform the old hunting park, the rather sad ground across which his father, Charles I, had taken his last cold walk to the scaffold in Whitehall. The springing ground for the design was almost the very spot where the scaffold was set up outside the Banqueting Hall: if some gigantic goose planted its foot on Horse Guards, its splaying toes dictated the vistas, which were lined out with lime trees along the present Mall and Birdcage Walk, the central one on a canal, 33 yards (30 metres) wide, 930 yards (850 metres)

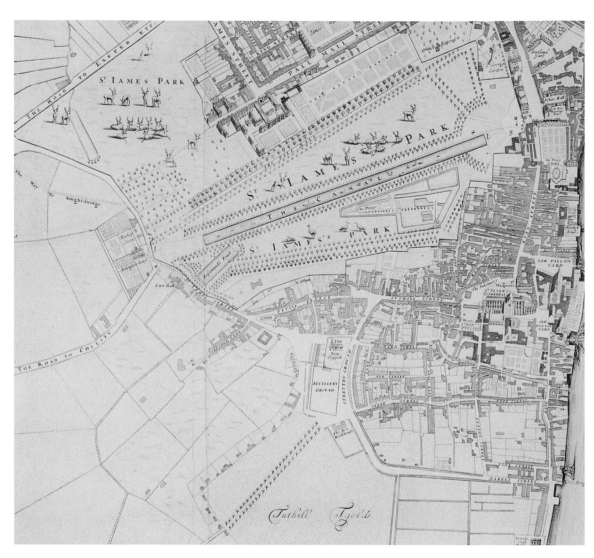

St James's Park. A detail from Morgan's survey of 1682, showing the completed layout of lime avenues and the canal pointing towards Arlington House and its gardens. St James's Palace is between 'Pall Mall Street' and 'The Pall Mall'. Spring Garden, the original home of the Admiralty summer house, is at the top right.

John Evelyn (1620–1706). Engraving after the portrait by Robert Nanteuil (1623–78). RCIN 806818

long, which extended from Horse Guards Parade to 'Rosamund's Pond'. This spring-fed pond, shaded by lofty elms 'round some of which were commodious seats for the tired ambulators to refresh their weary pedestals ... Where a parcel of worn-out Cavaliers were conning over the Civil Wars ... with pleasing reflections on their youthful actions',[17] was allowed to remain. Most significantly of all, as Morgan's survey map of 1682 clearly reveals, The Mall vista ended neatly on Lord Arlington's house.

This accident of design, which introduces an inevitability into the Buckingham Palace story, was perhaps not immediately apparent in the jollity of it all, as St James's Park seemed bathed in the sunlight and gaiety of the Restoration. There the King walked with his subjects. 'I had a fair opportunity of talking to His Majesty', wrote John Evelyn, keen to promote the work of the woodcarver and 'incomparable artist', Grinling Gibbons, 'and thence walked with him through St James's Park to the garden.'[18]

In winter there was skating on the canal, in fine weather the King, 'His shape so lovely and his limbs so strong', played *Jeu de Mail*, a vicious kind of croquet, on The Mall, which was surfaced in powdered and rolled cockleshells.[19] There were also the entertaining antics of the wildfowl, the King's pelicans, the osprey and tufted ducks, and the deer 'spotted like leopards', the antelope, Guinea goats and Arabian sheep noted by Samuel Pepys.[20] Evelyn observed the milk-white ravens, storks and a crane with a jointed artificial leg made out of a wooden box by a soldier.

Life in the Park was celebrated, at some length, by the poet Edmund Waller (1606–87):

For future shade young trees upon the banks
Of the new stream appear in even ranks;
The voice of Orpheus or Amphion's hand
In better order could not make them stand;
May they increase as fast and spread their boughs,
As the high fame of their great owner grows! …

Methinks I see the love that shall be made,
The lovers walking in that amorous shade;
The gallants dancing by the river's side,
They bathe in summer and in winter slide.
Methinks I hear the music in the boats,
And the loud echo which returns the notes;
While overhead a flock of new-sprung fowl
Hangs in the air and does the sun control,
Darkening the sky; they hover o'er and shroud
The wanton sailors with a feathered cloud.

Beneath a shoal of silver fishes glides,
And plays about the gilded barges' sides;
The ladies, angling in the crystal lake,
Feast on the waters with the prey they take;
At once victorious with their lines, and eyes,
They make the fishes, and the men, their prize.[21]

Another observer was John Wilmot, Earl of Rochester (1647–80):

… Unto this all-sin-sheltering grove
Whores of the bulk and the alcove,
Great ladies, chambermaids and drudges,
The ragpicker and heiress trudges.
Carmen, divines, great lords, and tailors,
Prentices, poets, pimps, and jailers,
Footmen, fine fops do here arrive,
And here promiscuously they swive … [22]

When the park gates closed, the stuff of Restoration comedy continued in the Mulberry Garden, where John Dryden (1631–1700) enjoyed the house speciality, mulberry tarts. William Wycherley (c.1640–1716) in *The Humourists* makes his character Friske ask 'Why does not Your Ladyship frequent the Mulberry Gardens oftener?' and another character comment 'It was very full, Madame, of ladies and gentlemen who made love together till twelve o'clock at night.'[23] Lord Arlington took over, acquiring a 99-year lease on the garden in 1677 and closing it down. Lord Goring's dream garden was reassembled once more, this time for good.

In 1673 Arlington, powerful as he was, had been accused of 'popery' and his wife of spying; the King could not afford to lose him so he was in no real danger, but he was forced to leave London and during his absence his house burned down. John Evelyn went to see the damage on 21 September 1674, reporting that hardly anything was saved. Undeterred, Arlington rebuilt, having finally secured the freehold from the Davies trustees in 1677. The new Arlington House was turned around, to face eastwards along the St James's Park Mall.

For the last eight years of his life, from 1677 until 1685, Arlington spent lavishly on his garden. He was unstinting in the legacy he planned for his daughter and son-in-law, the young Duke and Duchess of Grafton. John Evelyn became a close friend of the family during these years, even visiting Duchess Isabella when she was 'great with child' in September 1683, frequently dining and sleeping over at Arlington House, and being fetched from his home at Sayes Court, Deptford, by Arlington's coach to visit Euston Hall. Evelyn is known to have contributed to the gardens at Euston, between the hawking and hunting expeditions, and so it seems perfectly likely, given the

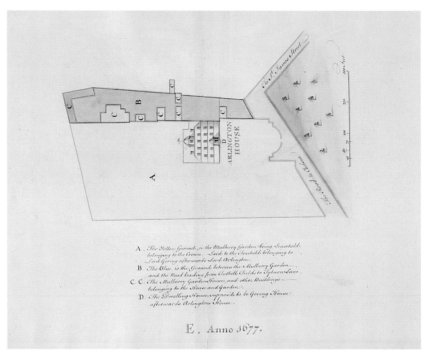

Arlington House. An early 20th-century collotype of a 17th-century original. RCIN 702808a

Copy of a plan of 1677 of Arlington House from the indenture, The Queen's Palace and Richmond. RL 18911

way that garden-makers and gardeners converse in each other's company, that Arlington House had the Evelyn touch. During these years, Evelyn was tussling with his great unfinished 'compendium of horticultural lore and practice', his *Elysium Britannicum*.[24] Arlington's protégé, the poet John Dryden, celebrated the outcome of their gardening friendship:

> The beautious gardens charm the ravish'd sight,
> And surfeit every sense with soft delight; … [25]

Now that the garden façade of the house faced westwards it had a full-length terrace 'Where lovely jasmines fragrant shade supply', and the prospect, out across the Great Garden 'o'er villages and forests strays', was of the well-treed, if not actually forested, Hyde Park, Brompton and Chelsea. In a garden at the end of the terrace, orange trees in 'six of the greatest earthen pots' were set out; Evelyn was particularly keen on their cultivation.[26] The oranges had winter quarters:

> A dome whose walls and roof transmit the light;
> Here foreign plants and trees exotic thrive,

FAR LEFT From Marshal's *Florilegium*: orange (*Citrus aurantium*), *Crocus vernus* (left), *Crocus vernus* ssp. *albiflorus* (right), grass snake (*Natrix natrix*) and goat moth larva from folio 3. RL 24270

LEFT The lilies and 'the blushing rose' from the *Florilegium*, folio 90: *Rosa versicolor* (in bud and flowers), *Periploca graeca* (Virginian silk-vine, top centre), *Robinia pseudacacia* (top right), *Hesperis tristis* (sad dame's violet) and scarlet Turk's cap lily (with mullein moth larva). RL 24357

Sir Godfrey Kneller (1646?–1723), *Isabella, Duchess of Grafton and her son*, oil on canvas, *c*.1673.

> And in the cold unfriendly climate live;
> For when bleak winter chills the rolling year,
> The guarded strangers find their safety here;
> And Fenc'd from storms and inclement air,
> They sweetly flourish ever green and fair;
> Their lively buds they shoot, and blossoms show,
> And gaily bloom amidst surrounding snow.

Poetic lovers could

> … spend the flying hours in amorous joy
> Or through the maze forgetfully they stray
> Lost in the pleasing sweetly winding way …

And Dryden seems quite in love with the flowers:

> A thousand flowers of various form and hue
> There spotless lilies rear their sickly heads,
> And purple violets creep along the beds;
> Here shews the bright jonquil its gilded face,
> Join'd with the pale carnation's fairer grace;
> The painted tulip and the blushing rose
> A blooming wilderness of sweets compose.[27]

Arlington also walled in the Great Garden, a 'field of meadow pasture … With thickset hedge at 27 feet [8 metres] inside the wall to preserve fruit trees from cattle'.[28] The greenery of these wall fruits – apples, quinces and pears – is clearly shown in the painting by Adriaen van Diest of *c*.1703. Some of Arlington's elms planted in the Great Garden survived into the twentieth century.

Arlington's son-in-law, the Duke of Grafton, died in 1690 from injuries received fighting in Ireland for William of Orange. His widow, Duchess Isabella and Countess of Arlington in her own right, retreated to Euston Hall with her 7-year-old son. She remarried; her

Adriaen van Diest (1655/6–1704), *Buckingham House and garden from Constitution Hill*, oil on canvas, *c.*1703. This painting remained with the Sheffield family until it was purchased by HM The Queen in 1991. It now hangs in Buckingham Palace. Westminster Abbey is prominent across the trees of St James's Park, and on the extreme right of the painting the beginning of Henry Wise's formal canal planted with seedling limes can be seen. The detail below shows how closely the walls were planted with espaliered fruit trees and shrubs. Note also the ornamental white wooden summer house attached to the wall. RCIN 404350

second husband, Sir Thomas Hanmer, was a great gardener. Arlington House was let and at some time in the 1690s there was another fire. The house was still 'sweetly sealed among gardens' but they were not so well kept; the orange pots were seen to 'stand abroad', being planted with indifferent evergreens, and other shrubs 'were not so bright and clean as farther off in the country, as if they suffered something from the smutty air of the town'.[29] In 1698 Arlington House was let on a repairing lease for six years to the Marquess of Normanby, and in 1702 he bought it for £13,000.

If there could have been anyone grander than Arlington it was his long-time political sparring partner John Sheffield, 3rd Earl of Mulgrave and Marquess of Normanby. As a young man he had had the temerity to woo the Princess Anne, daughter of the future James II, and had been banished for his pains (though soon forgiven). Now the Princess had become Queen, she gave him prestigious appointments and in 1703 made him Duke of Buckinghamshire and Normanby (usually abbreviated to 'Buckingham'). One of his nicknames was 'Lord Allpride'. His third wife, Catharine – the natural daughter of James II by Catherine Sedley, the daughter of the author of *The Mulberry Garden* – was called 'the haughty Duchess'.

On her exploration of London in the first years of the eighteenth century, the diarist and traveller Celia Fiennes had found Arlington House a very 'curious building' and at first she thought it belonged to St James's Park.[30]

Sir Godfrey Kneller (1646?–1723), *John Sheffield, Duke of Buckinghamshire and Normanby*, oil on canvas, late 17th century.

The builders' chaos of work in progress seems to have been the cause of this confusion, for in rebuilding Arlington's house to designs by William Talman – and changing its name – Buckingham was making a splendid forecourt, with a sweep of railing and ornamental gates by the ironmaster Jean Tijou, whose work can still be seen at Hampton Court. In the centre of his *cour d'honneur* was an octagonal basin and fountain with King Neptune riding his sea-horses. The only trouble was that the Duke had, once again, overstepped the mark. 'The Queen notes that the Duke of Buckingham, upon rebuilding his house, hath gone further into the Park than he had leave from the Queen to do,' the Surveyor General Samuel Travers was warned on 23 August 1703. Travers was to write to the Duke that 'Her Majesty expects him to comply with the leave given him, which as Her Majesty has declared was

Sutton Nichols (fl.1725–55), *Buckingham House*, engraving, 1731. The east entrance front facing St James's Park. The gates and railings are the work of the French ironmaster Jean Tijou. RCIN 702780

S. Torres (*fl.*1736), after J. Rigaud (1681–1753), *A Prospect of St James's Park (from Buckingham House)*, engraving, 1752 (published 1794). RCIN 702577

Sir Godfrey Kneller (1646?–1723),
Queen Anne, oil on canvas, 1702–14.
RCIN 405676

only to take in a ditch and a little beyond a tree before his said house so as there might be a straight line.' Buckingham did not alter his court, but he was firmly admonished that his coach could not sweep out of his gates and all down The Mall as he might fancy, but only turn through St James's Mews (now Stable Yard) into St James's Street, thus not passing the Palace.[31]

But the Duke had another ruse up his sleeve. In 1704 Queen Anne appointed her trusted Royal Gardener, Henry Wise, Deputy Ranger (at £200 a year) of St James's Park and Green Park. Wise (1653–1738), who chose as his motto 'Be ye wise as serpents and harmless as doves', was kindly and firm and 'at the same time astute enough to make a fortune, laboriously earned'.[32] He was already working at Kensington and Hampton Court for the Queen, at Marlborough House for the Duchess of Marlborough (and about to start at Blenheim Palace on the nation's tribute-garden for the Duke), but Buckingham, with an initial retainer of £1,000, gained him for Buckingham House as well.

Wise was asked to remove soil from the north side of the Great Garden (presumably the spoil from the long formal canal of Talman's design which is shown in the van Diest painting and was similar to the St James's Park canal) and to raise a mound on the south side. This mounding may be seen in the engraving of Buckingham's letter to the Duke of Shrewsbury (see page 42). The intention was to protect the garden from the clatter and smells of the stables, but Buckingham's instructions make Wise the begetter of the Mound, to become famous in Queen Victoria's garden over one hundred years later.

Sir Godfrey Kneller (1646?–1723), *Henry Wise*,
oil on canvas, *c*.1718. RCIN 405636

BELOW Colen Campbell (*fl*.1715–25) published his
Vitruvius Britannicus or 'The British Architect' in
1717. Page 44, illustrated here, shows the elevation
of Buckingham House, humbly inscribed to the
Duke of Buckingham. The engraving shows the
balusters and statues on the roof, described in the
text below. Buckingham's view from his roof would
have been one of the finest London at the time could
have provided. RCIN 1150760–764.44 (detail)

Henry Wise, 'the last of the great English formalists',[33] planted the double avenue of limes on each side of the long canal and also an elaborate flower parterre over much of the former Mulberry Garden ground – of lavenders, roses, jasmines, honeysuckles, pinks, lilies and scented-leaved rosemary and sages, all easily supplied from his and George London's Brompton Park Nurseries, which were on the site now occupied by the Victoria and Albert Museum.

No sooner had Buckingham settled down to enjoy his house and garden, commissioning van Diest's painted view from Constitution Hill (named for Charles II and his 'constitutional' walks), than he was accused of snubbing society, of 'despising both Court and Country' by 'staying in town at a season when everybody else leaves it' by his political nemesis, Charles, Duke of Shrewsbury.[34] Interestingly, in feigning the simple life 'of a civilized man' in his own defence, Buckingham tells us a great deal about his garden. He spends most mornings in his rooms 'high, quiet, free from early sun' overlooking Green Park, 'the pleasantest park in the world'. He, like his coachman, hates going out in the mornings. He might walk on his roof – 'covered with smooth milled lead with balusters' – in the company of the statues of Apollo, Liberty, Equity, Mercury, Truth and Secrecy that danced around it, enjoying 'a far distant prospect of hills and dales, and a near one of parks and gardens'.

He guides us into his gardens, down from the house by seven steps to a gravel walk and onto a long terrace, running from north to south with a covered arbour at each end. From the steps a path, 10 yards (9 metres) wide, leads between two groves of tall limes (dating from Evelyn and Arlington's time) planted in 'several equal ranks' upon a carpet of grass. The path is ornamented with tubs of bays and orange trees. 'At the end of this broad walk, you go up to a Terrace four hundred paces long, with a large Semicircle in the middle, from whence is beheld the Queen's two parks [Green and Hyde Parks] and a great part of Surrey; then going down a few steps you walk on the bank of a canal six hundred yards [550 metres] long, and seventeen [16 metres] broad, with two rows of Limes on each side of it.'

The flower parterres have 'fountains and water works' and statues; 'from the biggest of these parterres we pass into a little square garden, that has a fountain in the middle, and two green houses on the sides, with a convenient bathing apartment in one of them; and near another part of it lies a flower-garden'. The kitchen garden is 'full of the best sorts of fruit' with walks 'for the coldest weather'. The Duke has a private door through his book closet and greenhouse, down to 'a little wilderness full of black-birds and nightingales'.

Over the entrance to Buckingham House the Duke had placed the inscription *Sic situ Laetantur Lares* – 'The Household Gods delight in such a situation'. On the garden side he had put his name and *Rus in Urbe*.

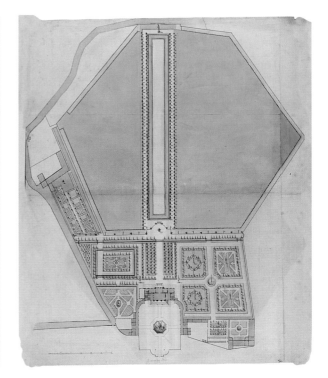

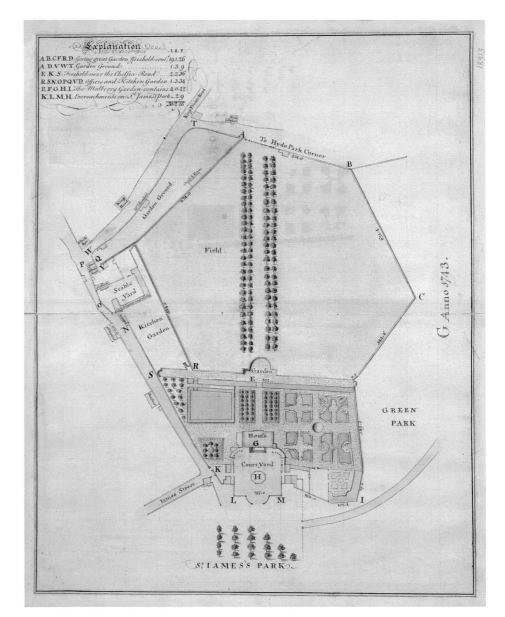

ABOVE Extract from an inventory (1743) taken after the Duchess of Buckingham's death, listing the contents of the greenhouses, valued at £107.

ABOVE RIGHT Buckingham House, c.1725. Watercolour plan attributed to Charles Bridgeman, showing the gardens at the highest state of formality as maintained by the Duchess after the Duke's death in 1721.

RIGHT Buckingham House, 1743. From the indenture, The Queen's Palace and Richmond, a survey drawing which suggests that the formal flower beds are giving way to grass after eighteen years. RCIN 1150274
Key:
A B C F R D Goring Great Garden freehold (19 acres)
[7.7 hectares]
A D V W T garden ground (about 1½ acres) [0.6 hectare]
E K S freehold near the Chelsea road (about 2½ acres)
[1 hectare]
R S N O P Q V D offices and kitchen garden (about 1½ acres)
[0.6 hectare]
E F G H I the Mulberry Garden (4 acres) [1.6 hectares]
K L M H encroachments on St James's Park (about ½ acre)
[0.2 hectare]

OPPOSITE A Plan of the Queen's Palace, watercolour on vellum, 1762, surveyed for the purchase by George III. The former 'Great Garden' has reverted to 'pasture ground' and the formal canal has been filled in. RL 29587

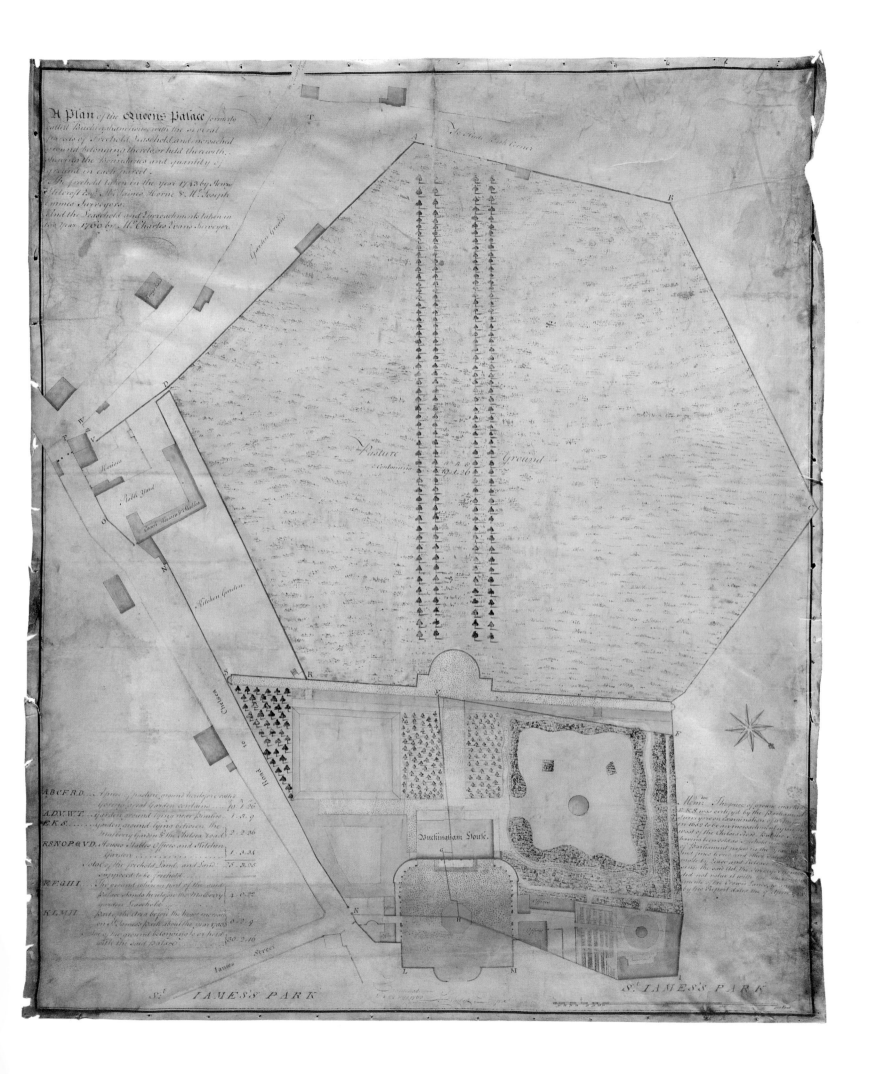

Buckingham died in 1721 but was survived by his Duchess until 1742. Their only surviving son, Edmund, was frail and lived in Italy, where he died in 1735, leaving a poignant codicil to his will expressing his wish to be buried in the garden or in the meadow at Buckingham House, 'where a little modest Tomb might be erected covered with a small open Temple which if well executed might be a beauty to the garden'.[35] The Duchess did not agree and Edmund, 2nd Duke of Buckingham, was buried in Westminster Abbey. When the Duchess was asked on behalf of Frederick, Prince of Wales – who remembered the enchantment of the nightingales – if she would sell her house, she replied that no one could possibly afford it.

After the Duchess's final departure the Buckingham heir, Sir Charles Sheffield, the 1st Duke's illegitimate son, continued to enjoy the house and garden until he became aware that at least half of his house, the north pavilion and half of his flower garden were sited on the old Mulberry Garden, for which his lease from the Crown had only a few years to run. The years ticked by, the young son of Frederick, Prince of Wales, became George III and Sir Charles Sheffield became inclined to sell.

By the time the former Buckingham House became the Queen's House the gardening fashion had changed: all the intricate geometrical flower beds, the fountains and mounts and formal canals were being swept away, and the English landscape style had taken the stage. Gardens were allowed to loosen their stays and imitate the flowing lines of the natural landscape. Edmund Burke (1729–97) had defined the sensations of beauty for the carriage-owning classes, opining that 'most people must have observed the sort of sense they have had, on being swiftly drawn in an easy coach, on a smooth turf, with gradual ascents and declivities. This will give a better idea of the beautiful, and point out its probable cause better than almost anything else.'[36] In 1753 William Hogarth (1697–1764) had published *The Analysis of Beauty*, with his praise of the serpentine line: 'a shallow, elegant, undulating double curve'.[37] A plain-spoken north-country man, Lancelot 'Capability' Brown (1716–83) had emerged as the supreme practitioner of sculpting grassy hills and vales, sinuously curving plantations of trees and expanses of water into the parks of his noble clients. A bevy of the lords for whom Brown worked – at Stowe, Petworth, Syon, Burghley, Warwick, Ragley and Alnwick amongst other places (the landscape craze quickly spread across the country by noble networking) – were determined that he should have a royal appointment, and in 1764 he was made Master Gardener. With the post came the responsibility for Hampton Court and St James's Park, and a handsome house, Wilderness House at Hampton Court, where Brown was to live for the rest of his life. Brown has detractors who blame him for destroying many formal gardens, but at Hampton Court he felt a professional pride in conserving William III and Queen Mary's Privy Garden; one of his legacies is the Black Hamburg grape he planted, now known as the Great Vine.[38]

Most of Brown's time was spent at Hampton Court, Richmond and Kew, where he became a familiar figure to the royal family, but immediately upon his appointment he had also designed schemes for St James's Park and the Queen's House gardens. In the Park he proposed replacing the formal canal with a long lake, retaining the lime avenues of Birdcage Walk and The Mall. His scheme was not carried out but was greatly to influence John Nash's redesign of the Park some sixty years later, and even today the lake, with its Duck Island, has a 'Brownian' character.

In the last decade of the eighteenth century the Queen's House garden was enlarged to its present size by the realignment of Constitution Hill and by taking in some miscellaneous properties that bordered what is now Grosvenor Place. George III wanted to buy more land on this western boundary to protect the garden, but the Treasury would not agree to the extra expense. When the tall houses along Grosvenor Place were eventually built, their view of the royal garden was a prime selling point.[39] In the 1760s Brown, living up to his nickname of 'Capability', anticipated this need for privacy – it was, after all, a 'selling point' of the landscape style that boundaries should be thickly planted with belts of trees to confirm the security of a private paradise, even in the countryside. William Kent (1684–1748) had triumphed in this way with his design at Carlton House for

A View of the Garden &c. at Carlton House in Pall Mall, a Palace of Her Royal Highness the Princess Dowager of Wales, To whom it is most humbly Inscribed by Her Royal Highness's obliged and most obedient Servant John Tinney

Vue du Jardin de Carlton House, Palais de S.A.R. La Princesse Douairiere de Galles

A view of the gardens &c of Carlton House…, engraving by William Woollett, 1760, of William Kent's garden for Princess Augusta (George III's mother), giving an impression of the boskiness and seclusion aimed for at the Queen's House. RCIN 702850

the King's mother, Princess Augusta, with 'rural seclusion in an urban setting – perhaps the first of its kind and of a form familiar to all who enjoy the squares … of London today'.[40]

Through the belt of protective trees at the Queen's House, Brown designed a characteristic serpentine drive, gravelled to suit a lady's pony chaise or light open carriage, which offered the traveller a kaleidoscope of changing views of copse and meadow in sun and shade. A second, more complex design survives which shows Brown's skills at their most brilliant as he juggles greater massings of trees (each drawn individually) with three main open glades of lawns, the largest glade framing an unusual oval lake. This second design was an outstanding example of the peculiar artistry of the man they dubbed 'Dame Nature's second husband'[41] and his genius for making even a dull piece of rather flat land appear beautiful. Sadly, this scheme was not adopted – the unwarranted expense was inevitably a factor, but it was most likely because of a personality clash between Master Gardener Brown and the King's architect Sir William Chambers (1723–96), who was in charge of work at the Queen's House. Chambers did not like Brown, thinly disguising his gibes at 'peasants [who] emerge from the melon ground to take the periwig, and turn professor'.[42]

Chambers had his own notion of where the inspiration for 'natural' design was to be found, gained from his early travels with the Swedish East India Company and his glimpses into the philosophy of Chinese gardening: he published 'A Dissertation on Oriental Gardening' in 1772, and was the authority on 'Chinoiserie', as the style became. He seems to have had the gall to adapt Brown's first design, changing the drive's serpentine curvings into rather wobbly meanderings of a vaguely exotic nature. The evidence comes from a plan of the 'jardin de l'Hotel de Buckingham à Londres' published in 1788 in Paris in *Jardins Anglo-Chinois à la Mode*, showing the drive's uncertain course through a plantation, with the whole central meadow fenced and home to what appear to be some curiously large and woolly sheep but are the Queen's Kashmiri goats. However, the serpentine pathway, shorn of the exotic tendencies of the pages of *Jardins Anglo-Chinois à la Mode* and possessing more 'Brownian' character, remains today as the frame of the garden.

Lancelot 'Capability' Brown, 'Dame Nature's second husband'. Engraving by John Keyse Sherwin (1751–90), after the portrait by Nathaniel Dance. RCIN 651444

RIGHT AND BELOW Lancelot 'Capability' Brown, landscape plans for the Queen's House, *c*.1762: the first scheme for a perimeter belt of trees and sheltered drive (RL 29593); and a more elaborate proposal for massed tree plantings forming glades, the largest having an oval lake. (RL 29594)

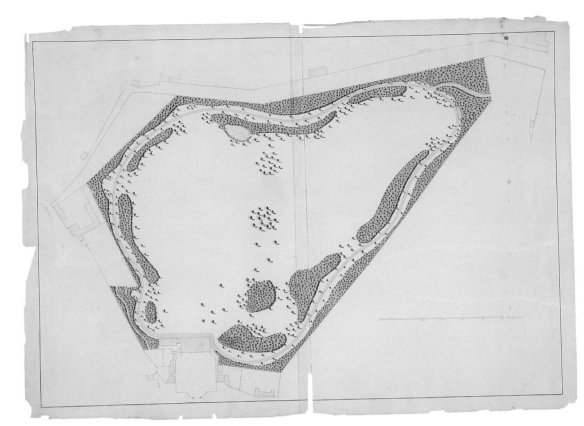

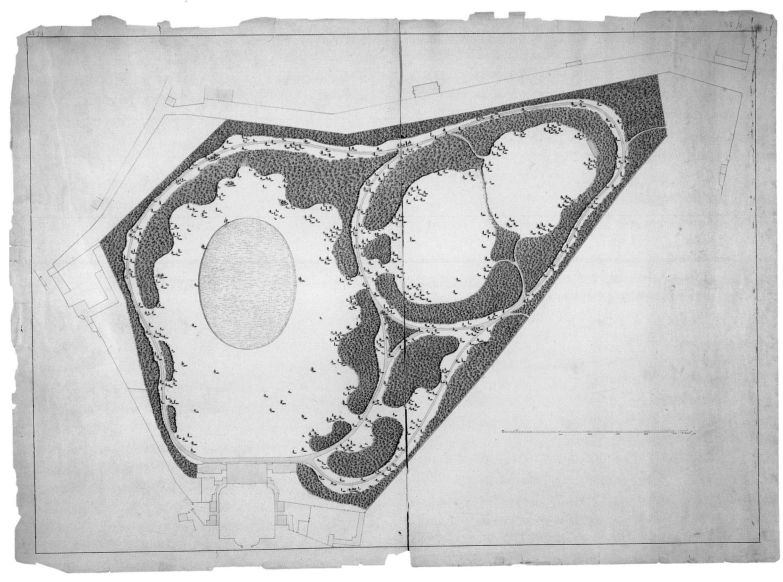

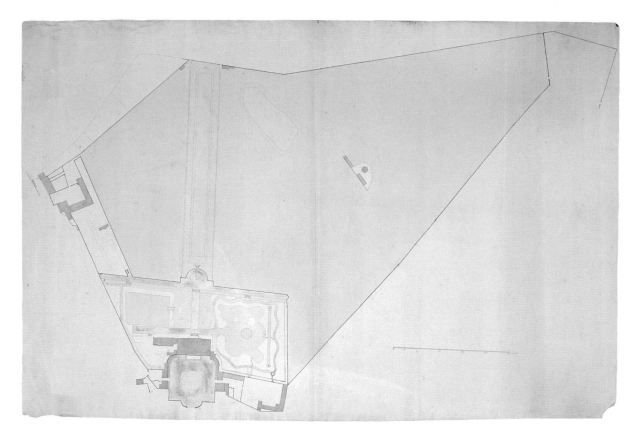

Detail of an anonymous plan of *c*.1763 showing the transformation of the formal garden into a 'wilderness' for Queen Charlotte. RL 29592

G.L. Le Rouge, *Jardins Anglo-Chinois à la Mode* etc., Paris, 1788, pl. XX., 'Jardin de l'Hotel de Buckingham à Londres'. Queen Charlotte's romanticised *jardin anglais* with Brown-style planting and drive around the perimeter of a paddock for Kashmiri goats.

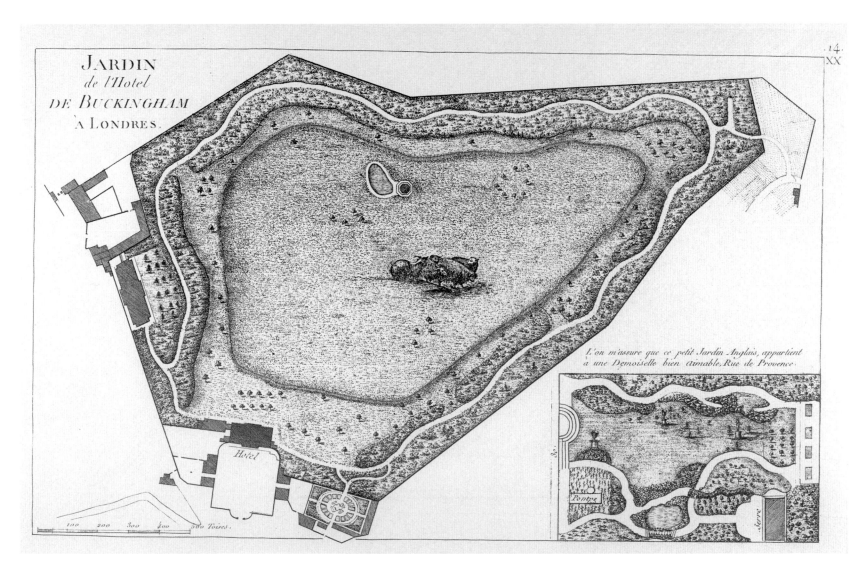

The serpentine driveway around the garden's outer perimeter as it is today, including plane trees and a hornbeam. The number and maturity of the trees in the garden play a large role in determining its ecological as well as its horticultural character – they provide cover, food and protection for the garden's rich diversity of bird and insect life, as well as baffles against traffic noise.

LEFT AND ABOVE The maples in the garden provide a particularly sharp, bright green in spring, as well as their better-known autumn colour.

ABOVE A waterfall of foliage on the
Mound, including *Acer palmatum*
'Dissectum' (the cut-leaved maple), and
a catalpa (Golden Indian bean tree) in
the centre. The flowers of hostas just
creep into the foreground.

RIGHT The copper beech on the left is one of
the earliest dated commemorative trees in the
garden, and was planted in 1902 by King
Edward VII and Queen Alexandra. The very
sharp-eyed may just be able to make out a
heron, lurking on the far side of the lake.

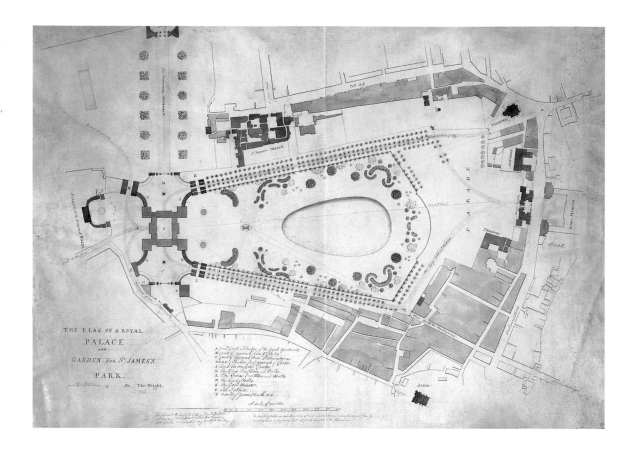

Another reason for this understated design was the ongoing debate and speculation about a new royal palace. George III disliked the dusty and dark recesses of old St James's and though the Queen's House served as a royal nursery, it was not thought large or grand enough for the principal town residence. Schemes for new palaces were scattered throughout the later eighteenth century and into the nineteenth: in 1766 it was to be in St James's Park, with a court of royal apartments and private gardens around an egg-shaped lake, designed by Thomas Wright. Palace sites were mooted for Green Park, on Constitution Hill and at Stanhope Gate on Park Lane; and the pipe dreams culminated in Sir John Soane's massive, Blenheim-like design for Hyde Park of 1821. Soane (1753–1837), architect of the Bank of England, had been nursing an ambition to build a palace for forty years; his Palace in the Park was possibly a retort to the Prince Regent's persistent favouring of John Nash (1752–1835), but it was too late. Queen Charlotte had died in 1818 and her house was empty. George III had breathed his last in January 1820 and the Prince Regent, now George IV, nearing 60, overweight, unwell, dependent upon cherry brandy and Lady Conyngham, having waited so long for his throne, declared he was 'too old to build a palace'. He recalled his childhood happiness at his mother's house and decided to have his 'pied-à-terre' at 'Buckingham House', which Nash would rebuild for him.[43]

The new King was a sad shadow of the once vivacious Prince who knew style and fashion when he saw them and had loved fine gardens; that term 'pied-à-terre' boded ill. Cruel time had also robbed the garden world of the one man, Humphry Repton (1752–1818), who might have persuaded him otherwise. Repton and Nash had once been partners and were considered 'the cleverest men in England' but they could not bite their tongues and work together.[44] Repton, longing for royal patronage, had prepared one of his Red Books of designs in the Indian manner for the Royal Pavilion at Brighton, and the Prince (as he then was) had told him, 'Mr Repton I consider the whole of this book as perfect',[45] and promised to have every part 'carried into immediate execution'. A game of cat and mouse followed, and eventually Repton realised that his erstwhile partner Nash was building and making the garden at Brighton using many of the Red Book ideas. Repton's *Fragments on the Theory and Practice of Landscape Gardening*, published in 1816, was dedicated to the Prince, but pointedly in praise of a 'historically minded, public spirited nobility' who forwarded the art of landscape design.[46] Repton had died in 1818, his practice inherited by his son, John Adey Repton, who had neither the energy nor the inclination for a royal appointment.

RIGHT Sir Thomas Lawrence (1769–1830), *George IV*, oil on canvas, 1821. This magnificent and flattering portrait shows the Table of the Grand Commanders to the left. RCIN 405918

FAR RIGHT Sir Edwin Landseer (1802–73), *John Nash*, pen and ink caricature, 1830.

BELOW A photograph taken in the 1880s of Nash's garden front of the Palace, clearly showing the richness of the decoration and the number of figures that originally adorned the parapet and the roof. Nash designed three conservatories for the garden front, but the one outside the private apartments was subsequently removed to Kew Gardens. RCIN 2101825

Joseph Nash (1809–78), *Buckingham Palace from St James's Park with the Marble Arch as the grand entrance*, watercolour, 1846. The Arch was dismantled and removed to its present site at the top of Park Lane the following year. RL 19892 (detail)

The King, knowing the brittle vanities of garden designers, now used Nash (who had the additional kudos of his appointment as official architect to the Office of Woods and Forests, the government's guardians of royal residences) for almost everything. Nash too was an old man, aged 73 when he began work on Buckingham House, and still with the responsibilities of his great ceremonial route from Regent's Park to The Mall, of building Clarence House and a new Royal Stand at Ascot, and the development of the Carlton House Terraces.

Almost sixty years had passed since Brown's abortive design; the oaks, limes and elms planted by Lord Arlington and the Duke of Buckingham had merged with the younger, but faster-growing, pines and evergreen shrubs of Chambers's scheme, and the garden had assumed the appearance of a rather dull park. At least Nash must have walked the ground, for he wanted to build a new Buckingham Palace, as it was now called, on the slightly higher north side next to Constitution Hill. The low, marshy nature of the actual site had always been a problem, for the springs of the old Tybourne still ran in wet weather, and the cellars of Buckingham House were frequently flooded, being below the high-water mark of the River Thames at spring tides. Nash saw two ways to ameliorate these problems: being forbidden to rebuild on the higher site, he would have to excavate and raise the basement levels, building a new range of rooms along the garden front protected by a substantial terrace, and he would excavate a lake on the lower, southerly, side of the garden, to drain the surplus waters.

During the last five years of George IV's life Nash built his Palace: the Duke of Buckingham's brick house was encased and enlarged into a substantial U-shaped building of biscuit-coloured Bath stone, 'exquisitely detailed in a French neo-classical manner, making much use of sculptured panels and trophies, *oeils-de-boeuf* and carved festoons, while the principal feature of the garden front was a domed semi-circular bow'.[47] This serene garden façade remains much as Nash built it, sheltering an enfilade of splendid rooms – the State Dining Room, the Music Room, the White and Blue Drawing Rooms, and on the ground floor, the Bow Room, which gives access onto the terrace. At each end of the terrace Nash placed Ionic-columned conservatories with carved pediments.

The Marble Arch, conceived by the King as a national monument to the victories of Trafalgar and Waterloo, was to form the Grand Entrance onto The Mall. George IV was obsessed with Britain's victory over Napoleonic France, and one of his most prized possessions was the table of the Grand Commanders, made by the Sèvres factory for Napoleon and set with a ring of cameo portraits of his generals.[48] Out in the garden there was a more curious memento: a scion of the willow tree that grew over Napoleon's grave on St Helena was taken (prior to the removal of his remains to Les Invalides in 1840) and planted by the lake.

The garden's famous Waterloo Vase has a more complex history: Napoleon had seen the marble in the block, newly cut at Carrara in Tuscany, when he was setting out on his Russian campaign. He ordered a gigantic vase to be made which would be decorated with scenes from his intended victory, a plan which foundered in the Russian snows. After the final defeat at Waterloo, the partly formed vase came to Britain and to George IV via the Ambassador Lord Burghersh and a grateful

A weeping willow on the lake today. Willows are not necessarily long lived, but undoubtedly the sprig of the willow from Napoleon's grave on St Helena, planted in the reign of George IV, will have had its descendants in the garden. The oak tree to the left of the willow is said to have been planted on the spot where two unexploded bombs were safely detonated during the Second World War.

Grand Duke of Tuscany. In 1820 the King commissioned Richard Westmacott (who also carved the reliefs on the Marble Arch) to finish the vase, which was to have a place of honour in the Waterloo Chamber at Windsor Castle. In Westmacott's reliefs horses and men sweep around the vase in scenes of victory and defeat – 'groups of warriors, sufficiently distinguished in countenance and habiliments, bravely combating for the palm of victory'. Wellington and Napoleon are portrayed as victor and vanquished, but only as participants in the general scene. Westmacott is said to have been aware of the classical precedent of King Darius, whose invading Persian army took a block of marble for their victory monument with them into Greece; after the Persian defeat the Greeks purloined the marble and had it carved into a statue of Nemesis, the goddess of vengeance and fate.[49] The vase was much praised for its aptness and solemnity without triumphalism: its allegorical highpoint is with the figure of Europe 'having taken refuge at the throne of England, and joyfully rising at the approach of Peace, who is presenting the palm leaf to his Majesty, whilst Harmony and Plenty spread their influence around him'.[50]

The Waterloo Vase, for which the Borghese and Medici Vases were also inspirations, is larger than both of them – nearly 5.5 metres (18 feet) high, nearly 3 metres (9 feet) across and weighing around 40 tonnes (39 tons). It was found to be too heavy for any of the planned positions within Windsor Castle and William IV presented it to the nation in 1836; first placed in the National Gallery, it was brought to the garden at Buckingham Palace in 1906.

An interestingly battered plan of the 'Royal Gardens and Ornamental Water of the new Palace in St James's Park' survives, showing Nash's U-shaped Palace and a new, amoebic, three-tongued lake. The corner with the date has gone, but the uncertainty about the name of the 'new Palace' (there is no mention of the revival of 'Buckingham') suggests 1825, the date of Nash's estimate of £22,290 for garden works. There is no evidence that this was accepted, and with costs rising inside the Palace, it is likely that work on the garden relied on the direct, piecemeal labour already 'on site'.

Nash planned a broad lawn terrace on the north front for the private apartments, but this was whittled down to a narrower gravel sweep. The lake was apparently dug between 1827 and 1828, but proved so shallow, muddy and weedy that it was proposed to fill half in again a few years later. It was all most unsatisfactory.

The Palace had assumed the guise 'of a national monument as well as a house for a King',[51] and its future was assured. George IV died in 1830, Nash was sacked the following year for 'gross economic mis-management',[52] but work continued on the Palace for William IV, although he never lived there. The scandal of the vast expenditure and the building's perceived shortcomings drew some people's attention to the fact that the garden was in an unfinished state. 'Sorry we are to say that the place is unworthy of a suburban cottage', yelped one of the more extreme critics, George Glenny, the editor of the *Gardeners' Gazette*: 'The grounds themselves are barely decent close to the house', the conservatories are in a 'wretched state ... one is partly filled with scrubby old plants ... the other of old damaged furniture ... the one being enriched with buggy plants, and the other with buggy beds'. Worst of all were the gardeners – a 'vulgar, dirty, ragged set of beings employed as labourers' and underpaid for the task.[53]

Another view came from a landscape gardener named Jonas Dennis, in a small book of 1835 entitled *The Landscape Gardener; comprising the History and Principles of Tasteful Horticulture*. Mr Dennis appreciates that 'seclusion ought to be, and very correctly has been, the grand object of the designer of this interesting spot' but does not trouble to enquire into the designer's name. He is much keener to

ABOVE *A Plan of the Royal Gardens and Ornamental Water of the New Palace* (St James's Park), *c.*1825, showing Nash's proposals for the garden.

LEFT I. Hume (*fl.*1820), etching from *The Palace that N... built*. A copy of this book, preserved in the Royal Library at Windsor, contains thirty humorous illustrations of George IV and his new palace.
RCIN 702820

OVERLEAF Coloured lithograph of the lake and Nash's garden front from *The Landscape Gardener* of 1835 by Jonas Dennis.

Caleb Robert Stanley (1795–1868),
*The garden front of Buckingham Palace from
across the lake*, watercolour and
bodycolour, 1839. RL 19891

present the surprise element of the gardens – 'what no one who only is acquainted with the exterior of the place would expect to see within' – with romantic engravings of large trees fringing a gleaming lake, and 'all the character of a wild scene in a rural district'. He says that 'the whole of the space visible from the garden front of the palace is exceedingly well managed' and it is the farther regions that 'might be mistaken for the remains of an ancient forest and pool left in its natural state'.[54] This 'naturalness' – largely the work of Mother Nature and the passage of time – was emphasised as something truly remarkable in the centre of the city that London had become; in truth it might be concluded that the developers and speculator-builders whose streets stretched from the garden walls as far as the eye could see had played as important a part in defining the character of the garden as any creative designer.

The name of the man blamed by the venomous George Glenny, and equally praised for his 'fine taste' by Mr Dennis, was William Townsend Aiton (1766–1849), the Royal Master Gardener

who had succeeded his father, William Aiton, after his death in 1793, just as Aiton senior had earlier succeeded Lancelot Brown. William Townsend Aiton had collected onerous responsibilities for most of the royal gardens; he had worked at Carlton House and Brighton Pavilion; and Kew, Windsor, Kensington Palace and St James's were all his province. George IV had relied upon him and he had attended the King almost daily at Windsor, driving in his gig from his official house at Kew and 'if for any inadvertent reason he was prevented for two or three days, a mounted dragoon carrying a message from the King was sure to be seen early in the morning at his house'.[55] Aiton's loyalty and hard work were recognised by his appointment as 'Director General of His Majesties Gardens' in 1827, and Buckingham Palace was added to his lot. He must have started to implement Nash's plan but was expected to do far too much in all the gardens, from designing ornamental buildings to finding and prosecuting the petty pilferers amongst his gardeners, from organising and paying for (out of his own pocket until his expenses were repaid by the Treasury) the planting at Royal Lodge to after-hours' revising of his father's *Hortus Kewensis*, as well as all the travelling involved. William IV abolished the Director's post and relieved Aiton, who was by this time 65, of everything except Kew, Richmond and Buckingham Palace.

So, once again, the garden was in the hands of an old man, one looking to his retirement (on a comfortable royal pension of £1,000 a year), and not inclined to the grand vision. Aiton was trained as a landscape gardener, but for his whole career he had been engrossed in the earthy domesticities of gardening, the niceties of being an horticultural courtier, and – if he had ever possessed the vision of a Brown or a Repton – it had become mossy with age. Old men and ancient trees have fellow feelings, neither wishing to disturb the well-earned tranquillity of the others.

Aiton was the last chance for Buckingham Palace's garden to have yielded to the touch of harmonious design: Nash, after all, had achieved 'a building of great originality and distinction',[56] with interiors that, in the opinion of the Palace's architectural historian John Martin Robinson, 'stretched the eighteenth-century classical tradition to its limits to create an aura of extreme opulence'.[57] Such opulent classicism reigned in the great houses of the King's subjects – at Stowe, Holkham, Blenheim and countless others – which found their immortal corollary and abiding confidence in the harmonious dispositions of massings and voids, the counterpoints of light and shade, that made up the English landscape style. No one seems to have recalled the brilliant seclusion of Kent's Carlton House garden, nor even the plan by Lancelot Brown; or is it more likely that they thought that such a garden was hardly necessary for a slip of a girl? The old men ordered a tidying-up and the planting of a few flower beds – surely enough to please the 'poor little Queen' with a 'task laid upon her from which an archangel might shrink' and yet of 'an age at which a girl can hardly be trusted to choose a bonnet for herself'.[58]

E. Bristowe, after John Cox Engleheart,
William Aiton, oil on canvas, n.d.

2

'*a solitary walk in the garden ... with my umbrella as companion*'

FROM THE DIARY OF KING GEORGE V, 22 FEBRUARY 1912

2

PRECIOUS PRIVACY
George III to King George VI

The Wellington Arch at Hyde Park Corner. The azaleas, cherries and other flowering shrubs coming into full bloom in the foreground are amongst the many spring-flowering species planted in the garden during the 1930s and 1940s for King George VI and Queen Elizabeth. However, the magnolia cultivar 'Elizabeth' was presented by the Brooklyn Botanic Garden to HM The Queen in 1982.

THAT DELICIOUS GOSSIP Horace Walpole (1717–97) gleefully recorded that George II's Queen, Caroline – irked by the *beau monde* and *demi-monde* sporting themselves in St James's Park and Green Park – had asked his father what it would cost to regain the parks as private royal gardens. Prime Minister Robert Walpole (1676–1745) had sagely replied 'only three CROWNS, madame'.[1] Those four words reverberated down the years to remind everyone how precious the private garden of Buckingham Palace had become.

George III and Queen Charlotte had cherished their privacy: Horace Walpole noted how 'the King and Queen lived in strictest privacy attended absolutely by none but menial servants; and never came to [St James's Palace] but for the hours of *levées* and drawing rooms'.[2] Zoffany's portrait of the Queen, with her two small sons George and Frederick costumed as though their nurses had spent the morning with the dressing-up box, has a glimpse of the garden of shorn lawns and hedges, neat gravel paths and an egret peaceably pecking at grubs in the lawn. The little Princes were brought up as outdoors children, and they were observed at Kew in January 1765 by a young Scottish gardener, Michael Milliken: 'The Princ of Walls was all over the Garden esterday in a chise drawn by a mare and the other princ in the nurses armes for two hours' notwithstanding the cooldness of the day indeed they are fine Lusty Boys and do not fear the coold.'[3] There were thirteen more children to come and the garden must have been filled on fine days with growing children and their hoops and hobby horses.

Queen Charlotte was keenly interested in botany and gardening, though these were practised at Frogmore and at Kew rather than in London. Dr Robert John Thornton dedicated the 1807 complete edition of his famous *Temple of Flora* to her, and the exotic 'bird of paradise' flower, *Strelitzia reginae*, named in honour of the Queen, was celebrated with an enchanting drawing of her together with her flower and the Queen's House in *The New Botanic Garden* of 1812. The Queen took botanical drawing lessons at Kew from Francis Bauer and drew many of the plants from the garden. Her third daughter, Princess Elizabeth, decorated the upper room of Queen Charlotte's Cottage at Kew and the first-floor gallery at Frogmore with painted flowers and the Queen commissioned the flower painter Mary Moser, a founding member of the Royal Academy, to produce the floral compositions in what is now the Mary Moser Room at Frogmore. The Queen loved the picturesque in gardening, and her well-watered 35 acres (14 hectares) at Frogmore included a Gothic ruin, a thatched hermitage and her Temple of Solitude. Garden fêtes were held there during the 1790s, and George III's Jubilee of 1809 was celebrated with fireworks and a water pageant for 1,200 guests.[4] The Queen continued to use her London house until the end of her life but mainly for drawing rooms and levées, when courtly rituals were never diverted by the birdsong or sunshine of the garden.

William IV had so little regard for Buckingham Palace that when the Houses of Parliament were destroyed by a fire in 1834 he saw the opportunity of ridding himself of it. He proposed it

as the new home for Lords and Commons, not merely a temporary refuge because of the fire but as 'a permanent gift'. For the Houses of Parliament he saw it as 'the finest thing in Europe'.[5] It would undoubtedly have changed the geography of political London had it come to pass. Failing Parliament, the King hoped that either his beloved navy or the army could make use of the Palace.

Behind the bluff sailor King there was Queen Adelaide, the 26-year-old Princess of Saxe-Meiningen when he married her in 1818. It was a double wedding: two sons of George III, both well into their 50s, married two German princesses (the Duke of Kent to Victoria of Saxe-Coburg-Saalfeld) in desperate bids for an heir. The Kents successfully produced Princess Victoria; Adelaide's two daughters died very young and thereafter she devoted herself to being a model step-mother to the Fitzclarences, the children of the actress Dora Jordan (who had died in 1816).[6] William IV and Queen Adelaide had only seven brief years before the King died in 1837, and they used Buckingham Palace very little, preferring Windsor. Queen Adelaide was a loss to the garden for she was a truly knowledgeable gardener. She was particularly interested in growing florists' flowers — especially tulips, auriculas and carnations — and supporting the societies that were springing up to encourage city gardeners to try their hand at these, even if they had only a small back-yard. Several special varieties, including a pelargonium, were named for her. Queen Adelaide also

Johan Zoffany (c.1733–1810), *Queen Charlotte with her two eldest sons*, oil on canvas, 1765. The Queen with George, Prince of Wales, and Frederick, later Duke of York. Through the window may be glimpsed the garden of the Queen's House. RCIN 400146

J. Burke after Angelica Kauffmann, *Queen Charlotte at Buckingham House*, n.d. Inset at top left: Sydenham Edwards, *Strelitzia reginae*, the exotic flower named for the Queen as Princess of Mecklenburg-Strelitz, plate 53 from *The New Botanic Garden*, 1812.

patronised the flower painter Augusta Innes Withers, giving her the appointment of 'Flower Painter in Ordinary' in 1833. Mrs Withers was one of the most distinguished woman artists for another thirty years; a member of the New Watercolour Society and the Society of Lady Artists, she drew plates for the Horticultural Society and the *Pomological Magazine*.[7]

Offloading Buckingham Palace was a vain hope for William IV, for the house at the top of The Mall had acquired a symbolic rôle. For the young Princess Victoria, who was awoken at Kensington Palace early in the morning of 20 June 1837 to be told that she was Queen, it represented a rite of passage: 'I really and truly go into Buckingham Palace the day after tomorrow', she wrote to her Uncle Leopold three weeks later, 'but I must say, though I am very glad to do so, I feel sorry to leave for ever my poor old birthplace.'[8] It was the unfinished state of the Palace and especially the rubble and rubbish in the garden that made the gardening press her self-appointed champions and loud in their complaints: 'for our beloved sovereign to be unable to command of her lazy superintendents of gardens a bouquet fit for a queen, is highly discreditable and perfectly true', George Glenny thundered.[9] Here he had a particular interest as a champion of florists' flowers as his recently published *The Properties of Flowers* had become the standard for Florists' Clubs in Midlands industrial towns: he hoped for royal encouragement with pinks, tulips and polyanthus at the Palace, despite the London 'smuts'.[10] However, at first the Queen was happy enough with her flowerless garden because her closest companion, her spaniel Dash, was perfectly content with its spacious wildness.

Sir Edwin Landseer (1803–73), *Portrait of Dash*, oil on wood panel, 1836. RCIN 403096

Queen Victoria and Prince Albert after a Drawing Room at Buckingham Palace, 11 May 1854. Photograph by Roger Fenton (1819–69), coloured by Edward Henry Corbould (1815–1905).

In his biography of Lord Melbourne, Lord David Cecil saw a 'tranquil and garden-like atmosphere' in the young Queen's idyllic adoration of her first Prime Minister: they walked and talked and sat together in the garden a great deal. Lord Melbourne assured her (they were talking of worldly values) that it was natural that she should be bored by her gardens, 'for a garden is a dull thing'. Did he mean *her* garden was a dull thing? It may certainly have been flowerless, for every week he sent her a carefully chosen bouquet from his own lovely garden at Brocket in Hertfordshire. David Cecil extended the metaphor of the flowers: 'Their fresh fragrance symbolized the quality of his unchanging feelings for her; that feeling which so often brought the tears to his eyes and compelled him every now and then in the course of a conversation to bend forward and impulsively to kiss her hand.'[11]

The young Queen married Prince Albert of Saxe-Coburg and Gotha in the Chapel Royal at St James's Palace on 10 February 1840. The Prince, among his many interests and talents, had felt himself a gardener from childhood; he found the 'inward force and growth' of nature attractive, he appreciated the art of the gardener who 'devises a garment for a piece of ground and while it is growing he is able to polish, cut and carve and fill up here and there and to hope and to love'.[12] On a practical level, his reorganisation of the Royal Household brought the garden under in-house management and a head gardener, George Wyness, was appointed in 1840, a pleasant villa being built for him at the rear of the Royal Mews. Things immediately looked up. The Queen wrote to her Uncle Leopold in May 1841: 'We have lovely weather … We sit out a g^t deal in this pretty & most invaluable garden, w^h is so much improved, & sitting under the Lime trees in the shade with a pleasant breeze, is delicious.'[13]

The business of raising a royal family was already under way. Princess Victoria had been born in November 1840, and Prince Albert Edward followed a year later. The last of the nine children, Princess Beatrice, was born in April 1857. Once again the garden echoed to the sounds of a happy family of children, the lulling crunch of the perambulator wheels on gravel, laughter and squabbles over toys on the lawn, noisy family games of skittles, squeals of delight at the baby ducklings and of alarm when the Prince Consort's greyhound Eos chased the silver pheasants. The 'domestic daisy-chain' of garden life was a blessed balm to the life indoors, the state banquets, the fabulously costumed balls when everyone galloped to Strauss polkas, the virtuoso concerts, and for the Queen the relentless hours at her desk with her papers and the repeated agonies of childbirth. When she was approaching 70, on the eve of her Golden Jubilee day of festivities in 1887, she was to sit in her garden again and recall the times spent there in 'former happy days'.[14]

Back in those 'happy days' the garden was 'much improved' by the Prince Consort's eagle eye and by good gardening: the conservatories were filled with palms, ferns and pretty pelargoniums;

RIGHT Queen Victoria, pencil and watercolour sketch of Lord Melbourne with Islay. RCIN 980070

FAR RIGHT Queen Victoria, pen and ink sketch, captioned 'Alice walking in the Garden at B. Palace'. From Queen Victoria and Prince Albert's sketchbook, 1841–59. RCIN 980024

the lawns were well kept and made a green velvet edging to the lake. The lake, now properly dug and supplied with water, had a boathouse and an overgrown island left as a refuge for nesting wildfowl – for the Prince was very interested in wildlife, one of the many aspects on which he was 'reforming' the Queen's mind. His modernising also meant family photo-calls for the pioneering professional photographers he was keen to encourage. On 22 May 1854 the eight royal children, all beautifully dressed, were lined up for Roger Fenton's portrait in the garden. This assemblage was a landmark in photography, an early 'instantaneous' snapshot taken in seconds with one of the new glass-plate negatives.

Roger Fenton (1819–69), Queen Victoria, Prince Albert and their children in Buckingham Palace garden, 22 May 1854. From left to right: Prince Leopold; Prince Alfred; Princess Helena; Princess Alice; Albert Edward, Prince of Wales; Prince Arthur; Princess Louise; Queen Victoria; Victoria, Princess Royal; Prince Albert.

The Queen, as she grew older and her child-bearing was past, came to need cold fresh air constantly, she was 'always poorly and stupefied in hot weather'.[15] Prince Albert found Buckingham Palace 'stifling' (in atmosphere as well as temperature), and they both enjoyed the garden in winter – the royal round meant they were there early each year, usually in February. The colder the weather, the better. Winters seemed colder then, and the lake was shallow enough to freeze over: 'very severe weather w[h.] I delight in', wrote the Queen in February 1853. 'The snow enabled the Children to sledge down a Bank like a Montagne Russe & ... the ice has been so strong and thick that there has been delightful skaiting [sic].'[16] Victoria loved to watch her husband's accomplished pirouettes, but the ice was not always so safe, as the Prince Consort, writing to his sister-in-law, had cause to remember:

> The cold has been intense ... Nevertheless, I managed, in skating, three days ago, to break through the ice ... I was making my way to Victoria, who was standing on the bank with one of her ladies, and when within some few yards of the bank I fell plump into the water, and had to swim for two or three minutes in order to get out. Victoria was the only person who had the presence of mind to lend me assistance, her lady being more occupied in screaming for help. The shock from the cold was extremely painful, and I cannot thank Heaven enough, that I escaped with nothing more than a severe cold.[17]

The 'Montagne Russe' (a term the Queen had learnt from the traditional Russian 'sliding hill' – a hill specially built for amusement in gardens such as at Tsarskoe Selo and Oranienbaum, imperial residences near St Petersburg) was the Mound, on the south side of the garden. The Mound's colourful history had begun with Henry Wise on the Duke of Buckingham's orders, as shown on page 42, where soil was dumped to stabilise the lowest and boggiest part of the garden. All available excavated material from the lake had been added, and on 27 March 1832 Hansard recorded a protest from the House of Commons as to 'the rubbish and filth from all parts' that were being taken into the garden to shore up the Mound. Or was it simply that the garden needed protection from the building development to the south, in the streets of Belgravia? The young Queen Victoria and Prince Albert, ever ready to make a virtue out of convenience, saw the Mound, beautified with evergreens and with a rustic pavilion on the top to give a view out over the lake, as their chief garden project. The Queen wanted 'a place of Refuge' and in July 1842 Prince Albert was informed that 'by attentions to economy' in the endlessly continuing building works the sum of £250 had been found, which it was hoped would be adequate.[18] By the miracles of royal persuasion, or perhaps additional funds when the time came, it was – though what the Prince achieved with this was astounding. It was not untypical that the authorities would spend half a million pounds and more on the Palace and begrudge £250 for the garden.

'Skating at Buckingham Palace', February 1895. From the
album of Princess Victoria of Wales, 1893–5.

H. Havell (fl.1803–37) after J. Burnet (1784–1868),
The Queen's House in winter, lithograph, 1817. RCIN 702801

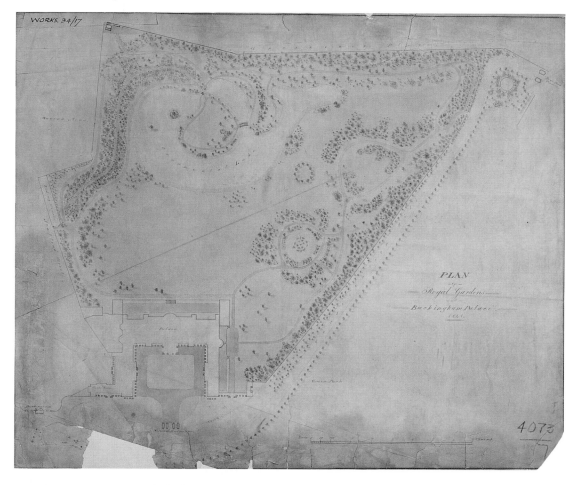

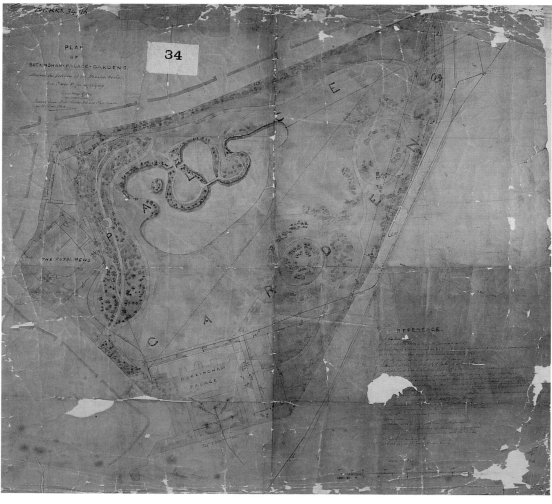

These Office of Works plans reveal the early Victorian garden. Top, 1841, shows the changing outline of the lake. The ice-house is at the Palace end of the Mound.

Below, 1844, is a garden plan showing the marine works: the lines for drainage and supply pipes and further excavations of the lake's bank (a thick blue line) to improve the water levels. The new Pavilion is clearly marked on the Mound.

These images may be compared with the 1855 plan on page 147 to see the improvements made by Head Gardener George Wyness.

The lake still freezes in the winter, although it would be a brave soul who would trust their weight to its ice, while among the first signs of spring in the garden are the daffodils in bloom around its edge and the willows coming into leaf (see following pages). During the spring the island is still a sanctuary for nesting waterfowl, and visitors are strenuously discouraged from disturbing them. This part of the lake was excavated at the behest of Prince Albert for wading birds. The beds of north-east American plants are in the background.

Two Canada geese make their way down to the water's edge. The old willow stump visible on the bank in the main picture (left) was allowed to remain to provide a valuable habitat for beetles and spiders. The floating 'island' on the lake was constructed to replace the willow as a nesting site, and has proved successful.

FOLLOWING PAGES The bases of four wooden piers mark the site of the boathouse, photographed by Henry, Duke of Gloucester, in 1914 (see page 110). The willow shown growing out over the water on page 91 is in the centre of the picture here, covered in new spring leaves.

ABOVE Gardeners removing the stump of an over-mature cherry by the lake, to make space for planting a new oak, *Quercus ellipsoidalis*. Planning for the long-term future of the garden is as important as its day-to-day maintenance.

LEFT The Wellington Arch from the lake. The yellow-stemmed ash, *Fraxinus angustifolia* 'Jaspidea' is just coming into leaf; see page 167 for its autumn colour.

Early summer and a bench provides an irresistible spot for contemplation. Who would believe that Victoria Station is less than a mile away? Here a family of Emperor geese, whose young will have been raised in the garden, can be seen under one of the garden's largest plane trees.

LEFT High summer: purple loosestrife
and flag irises have colonised the
margins of the lake.

ABOVE Dogwood and a balsam poplar on the island in their autumn
colours. In the autumn the colours of the leaves around the lake
and their reflections create an almost Japanese simplicity.

The designer of the Pavilion seems most likely to have been Edward Blore (1790–1879), who was well practised in both the practical and ornamental aspects of gardens.[19] Blore was employed at Buckingham Palace from 1831 to complete Nash's project, and worked there throughout the 1840s.[20] He was also the protégé of the novelist Sir Walter Scott (1771–1832), who was one of Prince Albert's heroes. It is likely that Prince Albert himself made a major contribution to the Pavilion's design. The timber Pavilion was adequately 'rustique', rather Bavarian in style, with a wizard's cap of a roof rising over the octagonal central room. Perched on its knoll and seen across the lake, with the distances given a little artistic licence, it easily gave the illusion of being in the Black Forest (or at least in Northumberland or Scotland), rather than Belgravia.

It was the interior of the Pavilion that was most remarkable, a product of the Prince's determination to encourage murals and the art of fresco in England (and apparently a trial for the decoration of the new Houses of Parliament) and the enterprise of maestro Ludwig Gruner, a scene painter and authority on Italian Renaissance frescos, who had become the Prince's art adviser. The central octagonal room, 15 feet (4.6 metres) high but rising to a dome, had a splendid fireplace flanked by gilded double doors; there were windows in the other five sides but otherwise no surface was left undecorated. Above there were eight half-circle lunettes depicting scenes from Milton's *Comus* – 'the shades of a trim garden devoted to the recreation of our Lady Sovereign'[21] – painted by distinguished Academicians, including Sir William Ross, Daniel Maclise, Sir Edwin Landseer, William Dyce, Sir Charles Eastlake and Clarkson Stanfield. One of the ante-rooms was decorated in the Pompeian style; the other illustrated the novels of Scott, with

scenes from *Ivanhoe*, *Kenilworth*, *Quentin Durward* and *Marmion* and Scott's favourite land-scapes of Melrose, Loch Etive, Lake Windermere and Dryburgh Abbey. Scott's novels were the Prince's favourites for reading aloud to the Queen.

The Pavilion, reached by gravel paths carefully graded for the pony chaise, was greatly enjoyed; for summer parties the crino-lined court ladies crowded the balcony to watch the boating on the lake, and in quieter times Victoria and Albert would make it the goal of their evening walks. But the Prince's enthusiasm was now directed to their new house at Osborne on the Isle of Wight, where he made lavish Italianate gardens and typically 'Victorian' plantings of cedars, wellingtonia, monkey puzzle trees (araucaria) and rhododendrons; it was there in the springtimes that the children did their gardening. After the excitement of the 1851 Great Exhibition he was busy with the purchase of the royal family's home in the Highlands, Balmoral Castle (they had leased it since 1847): the Queen was adamant that Albert should have complete charge at both Osborne and Balmoral, their private houses.

Albert's scientific bent led him to support what was still the Horticultural Society of London (founded in 1804), which had suffered a series of setbacks and scandals as the founding members (including the royal gardener W.T. Aiton) died. He oversaw the charter to the Royal Horticultural Society prior to the opening of the society's new garden at Kensington Gore, where on 5 June 1861 he planted a commemorative wellingtonia. It was to be his last public appearance; already ailing, overcome by the catalogue of griefs that had assailed the royal family that year, and worried in particular that the Prince of Wales was straying from the path of duty, Albert succumbed to typhoid and died at Windsor on 14 December.

Title page, The Decoration of the Garden-Pavilion in the Grounds of Buckingham Palace, *1845, engraved under the superintendence of L. Gruner (1801–82).* RCIN 708005

It is well known that the desolate Queen abandoned Buckingham Palace; that she clung to Albert's memory at Windsor and his tomb (which would also be hers) at Frogmore, and only wished to escape to 'his' houses at Osborne and Balmoral; that she took the Prince of Wales and Princess Alexandra of Denmark into the mausoleum for 'his' blessing the night before their wed-ding in St George's Chapel; that she observed, but took no part in, their wedding on 10 March 1863; and that the lovely Princess 'cast her eyes shyly down like a rosebud princess in a fairy tale', while

The Decoration of the Garden Pavilion. Cross-section of the Pavilion with planting, shown as plate 2 of this sumptuous publication. RCIN 708005

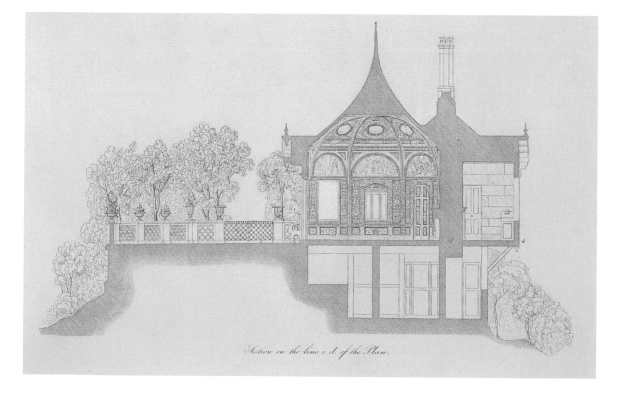

The Decoration of the Garden Pavilion.
The Walter Scott Room.
RCIN 708005

The Decoration of the Garden Pavilion.
The Comus Room. RCIN 708005

These 1880s photographs show two views taken from the verandah of the Pavilion, looking out over the lake. Some of the other buildings introduced into the garden by the Prince Consort and shown on contemporary maps as 'hides' and 'nesting boxes' can also be seen, hidden among the trees, while the willow growing out over the water in the 1880s (left) is still there today, its lower branches now completely submerged and in great demand as a nesting site by coots and moorhens. RCIN 21018329–30

FOLLOWING PAGES The Pavilion itself, emerging from the greenery on the Mound. RCIN 21018331

The balcony of the Pavilion at one of Queen Victoria's rare entertainments in the garden, as drawn for *The Illustrated London News*, 22 July 1871.

the black-clad Queen 'raised her eyes towards heaven with an expression which moved all who beheld it'.[22]

The Prince and Princess of Wales moved into Marlborough House in The Mall as their London home, and had as their retreat in the Norfolk countryside the Prince's beloved Sandringham, close enough to the coast for the bracing North Sea airs. Were this glamorous couple going to outshine the nervous, reclusive Queen, who occasionally opened her Parliament but was absent from London for whole years on end? In January 1869 the Prince of Wales wrote to his mother, 'the people – not only Londoners – cannot bear seeing Buckingham Palace always unoccupied', and a little later he suggested that she might come just for the day and drive in the Park: 'It is all very well for Alix and me to drive in the Park – it does not have the same effect as when you do it; and I say thank God that is the case. We live in radical times, and the more the *People see the Sovereign* the better it is for the *People and the Country.*'[23]

The Queen's absences cast a rather sinister pall over her 'dear garden', no longer a country garden but in the heart of an overcrowded city and suspect in itself: 'The situation is not healthy, the neighbourhood is poor ... be sure some future Sovereign, with more horror of malaria, or more regard to taste, will depute some future Mr Blore to condemn and discard it entirely', an anonymous correspondent had written to *The Times* when Blore was building the new east front.[24] The sluggish and smelly waters of the lake were a constant cause for alarm; the Queen's Physician, Sir James Clark, had reported it 'insanitary' in 1840[25] and part had been filled in. In 1855 it was suggested that it should be completely filled in and made into flower gardens, but the Chelsea Waterworks Company confidently promised an abundant supply of fresh water from their new reservoir at Hyde Park Corner, and two years later this was pronounced satisfactory. But malaria and typhoid were both endemic in London, both spread from infected water, and the death of Prince Albert only emphasised that no one, not even royalty, was immune. In summer the River Thames smelt like an open sewer and the stench drifted across the Pimlico streets to the Palace, which was so low lying that its own drains were far from perfect. In winter, when the stench might be lessened, the garden was down-wind of the smut-laden airs from the coal-burning houses of Brompton, Kensington and Belgravia (streets of fine houses faced in stucco so that they could be frequently repainted). One of the Queen's dressers,

The garden tools of the royal children displayed at the Swiss Cottage, Osborne, where they each had their own garden.

Frieda Arnold, who came from Germany, was outspoken about the filthy city air: 'Although the palace is surrounded by parks every time I come into my room my table is quite black, my armchair is speckled with little black particles and my lovely shining candlesticks are quite tarnished in two days. One can never leave any article lying about, and even in the cupboards everything gets dirty.'[26] It was the fog that crept uncannily through closed windows and doors, blackening the windows even on the insides, and in greenhouses and conservatories it was death to the plants. If that was indoors, how much worse was it in the garden? The fashion for spring and summer bedding-out arose precisely so that the tender bright flowers could make their brief appearances, and then be discarded when they were smutty and dying. Shrubberies of leathery-leaved hollies and laurels which could withstand the pollution became the dusty Victorian archetype in villa gardens from Muswell Hill to Penge, and in this the Queen's own garden at Buckingham Palace shared its horticultural difficulties with the gardens of her subjects.

In February 1867, driving to open the session of Parliament that was to pass the Second Reform Bill, the Queen had encountered some demonstrators amongst the usual cheering crowd, and the sea of 'nasty faces' caused her hurt and alarm. Bereft of the Prince Consort, she felt increasingly alone and nervous, and this too influenced her desire to stay in his 'safe' houses. During the following decade the garden's boundaries were reviewed and secured, with new gates and a *cheveux de frise* (protective iron railings taking their name from chariot traps) added to the walls. The belts of trees along Constitution Hill and Grosvenor Place were ancient, clogged with elm suckers, and badly in need of attention: the Master of the Household Sir John Cowell consulted William Brodrick Thomas (1811–98), thought to be one of the half-dozen best 'landscapists' of the day, who had worked at Sandringham for the Prince and Princess of Wales, substituting the formal gardens in front of the house for lawns and a watery rock garden. Thomas wanted to help but foresaw an immense task, clearing out the root-choked soil and dead trees and importing new soil to give new trees, including the smoke-tolerant London planes *Platanus x hispanica*, a chance. The Queen did not agree: 'Mr Thomas always wants to alter & change as he did at Sandringham', and she wanted 'no changes'. Sir John Cowell laboured away a little longer, enlisting the advice of a senior gardener at Windsor, who visited Buckingham Palace, inspected the tree belts and made his suggestions. Sir John then found

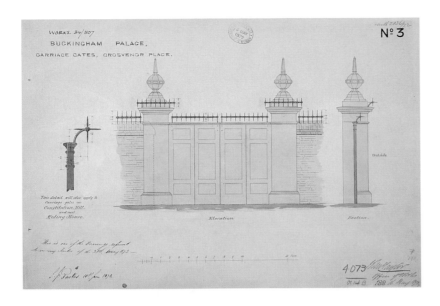

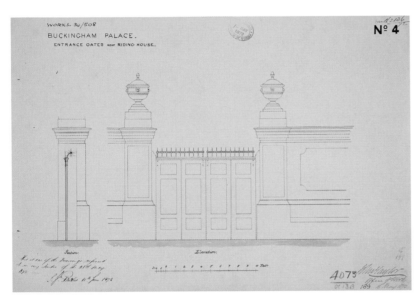

Office of Works drawings for the *cheveux de frise*
proposed for the Constitution Hill boundary
of the garden, 1872.

that the Queen had taken matters in hand and given her instructions to the Buckingham Palace
head gardener Edwin Humphreys (who had succeeded George Wyness in 1872).[27] Absentee
Queen she may have been, but her 'dear garden' was not entirely forgotten.

It was completely revived for the celebrations of the Golden Jubilee summer of 1887, and
just under two years later, on 20 March 1889, when a proposal that it should be opened to the
public was put to the vote in the House of Commons, it was defeated by 135 votes to 62. However,
Constitution Hill was opened to carriage traffic for the first time that year.

Then, in the spring of 1897, with the Queen-Empress's Diamond Jubilee being planned,
it was with a touch of imperial largesse that her Master of the Household, Lord Edward Pelham

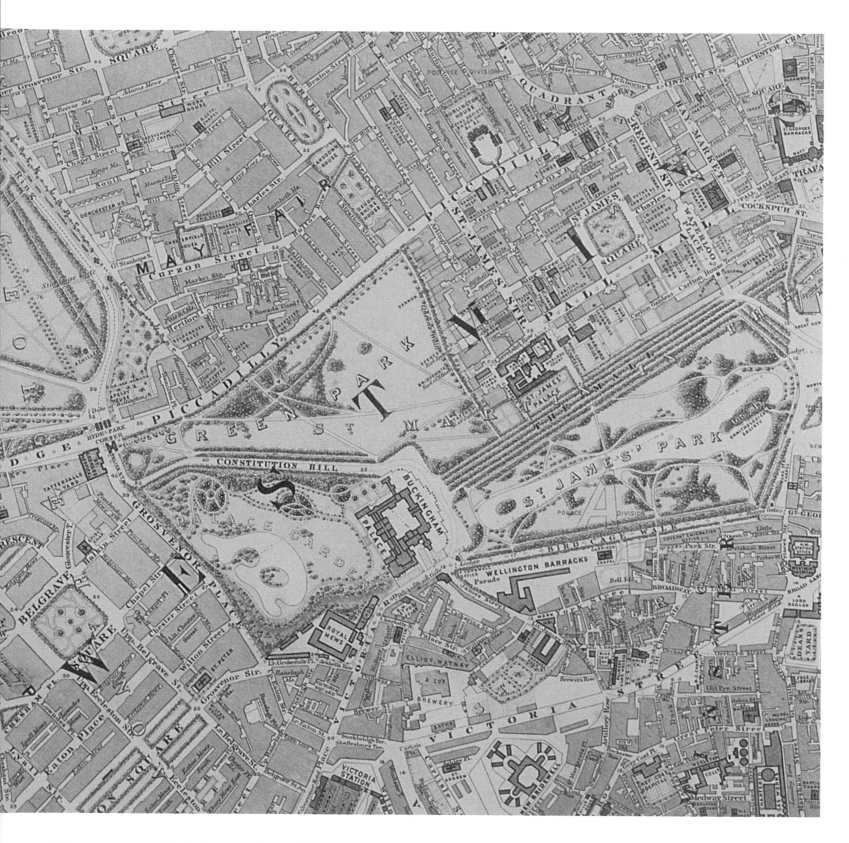

Clinton, gave *carte blanche* for the editor of the *Journal of Horticulture*'s celebratory feature on the royal gardens. It was a thorough job, pages and pages on the vegetable, fruit and flower gardens of Windsor which annually produced some 2,270 kg (5,000 lb) of grapes, 900 kg (2,000 lb) of strawberries, 550 kg (1,220 lb) of cherries and 450 large barrels of apples, and over 3,000 boxes of cut flowers as well as all the wreaths, bouquets and corsages that the Royal Household required. The journalists' first impressions at Buckingham Palace were of vast areas of lawns, water, shrubberies, and the 'enormous' Mound – 'we worked our way up by gravel paths, with their verges in grass, and richly we were rewarded by the arboricultural picture spread beneath us'. The London plane trees had become evident, but the elms were still fine, and there were laburnums, guelder rose,

Edward Stanford, Library Map of London and its suburbs, 1862. The map shows how the surrounding streets have become built up.

ABOVE The 'Round Bed' filled with Victorian bedding plants and protected by railings, photographed in the 1880s. In the background are what appear to be some venerable-looking elms. RCIN 2101832

RIGHT Frederick Morgan (1856–1937), *Queen Alexandra with her grandchildren and dogs*, oil on canvas, 1902. Queen Alexandra is shown at the kennels in the grounds of Sandringham with, on the left, Prince Edward (the future King Edward VIII) and Prince Albert (the future King George VI), and on the right, Princess Mary (later the Princess Royal). RCIN 402302

rhododendrons, azaleas, weigelas and lilacs, though there was still a lingering sadness that Her Majesty 'does not use it much' and it was not really *gardened*. The Round Bed was filled with pelargoniums, lobelias and calceolarias and the conservatory with zonal pelargoniums and palms, all ready for the Jubilee summer. Considering this was a London garden and the difficulties were well known, 'great credit' was due to Head Gardener John Stirling. Stirling had been in charge for some fifteen years, since Humphreys retired in 1883, and served his Queen until her death in January 1901.[28]

King Edward VII and Queen Alexandra were already grandparents when they inherited Buckingham Palace, and Alexandra was reluctant to leave Marlborough House, which had been her home for nearly forty years. It had often been mooted, politically, that they should have used the empty Palace earlier, but Queen Victoria had been adamant that they would not, and so for the new King it was more than ever a symbol of having reached his destiny, at long last. He oversaw a massive clearing-out and refurbishment, transforming the State Rooms to a 'sea of white and gold' in place of the Prince Consort's now dingy polychromy.[29] The private apartments were splendid and comfortable, the Queen's rooms 'remarkably beautiful and cosy', and the whole atmosphere was of freedom, comfort and luxury, refreshingly so amongst the courts of Europe.[30]

The garden, transferred to the care of the Office of Works so that a special labour force could be on hand for the big events – King Edward was notoriously impatient and exacting when he wanted something done – was also brought to a new pitch of splendour. The King and Queen planted a copper beech (*Fagus sylvatica* ssp. 'Atropurpurea'; see page 150) on the main lawn on 15 March 1902, not long after they had moved in. The horticultural world in general seemed to love the King for his passion for ceremonial tree planting, which he pursued wherever he went, doing 'more than anyone to popularise the pretty custom'.[31] He healed the fateful legacy of the Prince Consort's last public appearance as patron of the Royal Horticultural Society by becoming royal patron, with Queen Alexandra, in 1904, and subscribed £100 to the fund for the Horticultural Hall in Vincent Square, Westminster, which he opened. His love of flowers was genuine, an essential part of the King's expansive 'Edwardian' splendour, and was displayed in his enthusiastic support for flower shows, especially the Sandringham Flower Show, the Windsor Rose Show and the spectacular People's Palace Show at Mile End. Name plants were showered upon him, including a giant sweet pea of 'the richest

Behind the Mound, a surviving finial from Blore's façade, and a detail of one of the four rams' heads decorating its base.

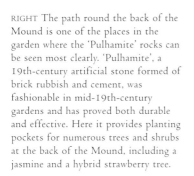

RIGHT The path round the back of the Mound is one of the places in the garden where the 'Pulhamite' rocks can be seen most clearly. 'Pulhamite', a 19th-century artificial stone formed of brick rubbish and cement, was fashionable in mid-19th-century gardens and has proved both durable and effective. Here it provides planting pockets for numerous trees and shrubs at the back of the Mound, including a jasmine and a hybrid strawberry tree.

and brightest crimson' named 'King Edward VII' and a pure white and 'prettily formed' Chinese primula called 'His Majesty' introduced by Sutton & Sons in 1905. He was especially fond of scented violets, lily-of-the-valley, gardenias and Malmaison carnations, the favourite and most fashionable flowers for the corsage, the small bouquet that the most beautiful women pinned to their bodices for every well-dressed occasion.

In his garden the King liked to see the blazing red pelargonium 'Paul Crampel', confirming the supreme status of this plant for dignified summer bedding, a fashion that seems to have started in Oxford and Cambridge college gardens, but which had the added virtue here of toning nicely with the scarlet tunics of the Guards at Buckingham Palace. 'Paul Crampel' is still the traditional variety par excellence for the Queen's Gardens around the Victoria Memorial. It also seems appropriate that the bulky splendours of the Waterloo Vase appealed to this King, so that he agreed to have it in the garden.

For Queen Alexandra, the Danish 'sea-king's daughter', it seemed equally appropriate that the Admiralty summer house with its adorning sea-gods was brought into the garden at this time. This small building was moved from the old Admiralty site in Spring Gardens at the end of The Mall. Though it appears to have been sur-rounded at first by delphiniums and other sea-blue flowers, the Summer house now looks out over rose gardens planted in the 1960s – the rose was Queen Alexandra's favourite flower. It was in June 1912, on the fiftieth anniversary of her first visit to England, that Queen Alexandra's Rose Day was instituted to raise funds for hospital and nursing charities: ten million pink silk or linen roses were sold on the streets of London by girls wearing white dresses with red sashes, reflecting the Danish national colours. Though the shy 'rosebud' Queen probably found it a tremendous ordeal to ride out in an open carriage and be showered with rose petals, she inaugurated one of the most enduring charity fund-raising campaigns of the twentieth century.

This was a peripatetic monarchy, highly visible, and Londoners were especially delighted at the constant comings and goings. The King and Queen spent January and February at the Palace, fulfilling engagements during the week and causing flutters of excitement around the countryside by their weekend visiting. After a holiday in the south of France and perhaps an overseas visit in the royal yacht *Victoria & Albert*, they were back at the Palace for the 'season' of presentation parties, investitures and mainly London engagements, then off to Windsor for Royal Ascot, a tour of the coun-try in the royal train, and more sailing during Cowes week on the Isle of Wight, as the prelude to the season's finale at Glorious Goodwood. Then the King went off to Marienbad spa while the Queen went to her family in Denmark; after that it was Scotland and Balmoral, before returning to Buckingham Palace. King Edward loved to be in London for the pre-Christmas theatre, operas and parties, where he was a real inspiration to the general cheerfulness; the worst weather did not deter him, and in one particularly thick 'pea-soup' fog his carriage was preceded and followed by a dozen run-ning footmen with flaring torches, a sight not witnessed since Regency days. Finally, the royal family gathered at Sandringham for Christmas.

Just as the King epitomised the energy and bonhomie of his 'Edwardian' age, so did many of the artists and writers around him, none more so than the architect Edwin Lutyens (1869–1944). The canopy now in the Throne Room at Buckingham Palace was designed by Lutyens, and prompts the idea that the final flourish for the Edwardian Palace would have been a Lutyens garden, surely with Miss Gertrude Jekyll masterminding the planting? It is too tempting a prospect not to be mentioned, but of course it was not to be, nor is there any suggestion that it was contemplated. The garden was now, with its serene lawns and trees, the ultimate luxury of the King-Emperor who had everything, except time. Most characteristically he would have spent a quiet hour fishing in the lake, thoughtfully stocked with trout as a present from the Earl of Denbigh.[32] Or he might have been glimpsed strolling with his beloved terriers, the Irish terrier Jack or his successor, the famous white fox terrier Caesar, the 'dog who could do no wrong'. It was Caesar's lot to follow his master's coffin through the streets of London, on the fine morning of 20 May 1910, in front of the German Emperor and eight kings.[33]

Sutton & Sons primula 'His Majesty', introduced in 1905 (pencil drawing reproduced in *The Garden*, 4 March 1905).

FOLLOWING PAGES A wintry shot of the rose garden and summer house, with the Jekyll-style catenary rope.

The small classical summer house, adorned with sea-god herms, was brought from the old Admiralty for King Edward VII and Queen Alexandra, and the *Wisteria sinensis* may date from their time. Spring pruning produces a froth of mauve racemes in May.

FOLLOWING PAGES The summer house seen across the Rose Garden, which was originally laid out by the rosarian Harry Wheatcroft in the 1960s.

Francis Byrne and Co., King Edward
VII with Caesar, photographed c.1908.

Once again there was unhappiness on the royal roundabout – 'musical palaces', though moving to the slow beat of the mourning drum, rather than being a lively party game. Alexandra would not be hurried out and the new Queen Mary was equally unhappy about leaving 'our dear belov'd Marl: Hse' for the palace of endless corridors where 'one can never find anyone'.[34] The new King apparently told Lord Esher that he would be happy to demolish Buckingham Palace, sell the site and use the money to enlarge Kensington Palace,[35] a remark reminiscent of Queen Caroline's bid to reprivatise the Royal Parks and about as practical: moving the Empire's focus and all the Household a mile or so westwards would surely have changed nothing.

However, Queen Mary loved gardens. She was the daughter of gardeners: her mother was Queen Victoria's cousin, Princess Mary Adelaide of Cambridge, who was married at the age of 32 to Prince Francis of Teck, the son of Duke Alexander of Württemberg. Princess Mary Adelaide was pretty, plump and popular, a familiar figure at Kew Gardens when she lived in Cambridge Cottage on Kew Green with her mother – and the court smart set referred to them disdainfully as 'the stout parties from Kew'.[36] Dr Joseph Hooker's folio volumes of gorgeous botanical illustrations of *Rhododendrons of Sikkim-Himalaya*, published 1849–50, were dedicated to Mary Adelaide. The Tecks were married in June 1866 and Princess Victoria Mary, always called May, was born a year later and followed by three brothers. Their father, created Duke of Teck, spent much of his time making a splendid garden at their home, White Lodge in Richmond Park, although as 'my parents were always in short street',[37] as Queen Mary later put it, they had lived economically in Florence for two years of her late teens. It was there that she acquired her love and knowledge of paintings, fine china and antique furniture, and of the wild flowers of Tuscany. Princess May had been swept into the royal family as the fiancée of Prince Eddy, the Duke of Clarence, Queen Victoria's eldest grandson and heir to the throne after his father the Prince of Wales. When Prince Eddy died of influenza in January 1892, May was the object of a wave of public sympathy, but she went quietly home to White Lodge. The younger brother, Prince George, soon to be Duke of York, had been low from a bout of typhoid fever at the time of his brother's death, but he became aware of May's strengths and virtues, and with a little royal ushering, she acquiesced to his proposal, and they were married in July 1893. It was to be a marriage of deep devotion and mutual respect, beautifully illustrated by the story Queen Mary's distinguished biographer, James Pope-Hennessy, tells of the wedding morning when Prince George accidentally caught sight of his bride 'down the long, long vista of one of the red-carpeted corridors of Buckingham Palace. He swept her a low and courtly bow. This gesture she never forgot.'[38]

As King George V and Queen Mary they journeyed to India at the end of their Coronation year, 1911, to preside over the Imperial Durbar at Delhi. For the King-Emperor it was 'the most wonderful & beautiful sight I have ever seen & one I shall remember all my life', but also an experience which convinced him of 'the dizzy and lonely heights' of his position. After the ceremonial the King went big-game hunting in Nepal; a 'mild tiger-shooting expedition' was arranged elsewhere for Queen Mary. Characteristically she took her knitting; she was quietly knitting in her tree-hut, waiting, when she pointed her needle – 'Look, Lord Shaftesbury, a tiger!' The tiger glared, the knitter returned a steady gaze, and the tiger loped off before his lordship had time to take aim. The King wrote her what amounted to a love letter from his camp: 'I am sure that I love you more each year & am simply devoted to you & loathe being separated from you ... With all my many responsibilities I feel that I want your kind help & support more than ever.'[39]

They arrived home in a snowstorm and drove to Buckingham Palace on a bitterly cold February day, the crowds, undaunted, cheering them to the echo. Reflection, and relief at being home again, seem equally mixed in the King's brief diary entry for 22 February 1912: 'went for a solitary walk in the garden ... with my umbrella as companion'.[40] The Queen was not far away, nor would she ever be, and both seem to have found an affection for the Palace, and especially for the garden, which was to shine through all the difficulties of the years to come.

Queen Mary, 'snapped' by Queen
Elisabeth of the Belgians
(1876–1965) on 7 May 1915.
From Queen Mary's photograph
album (detail).

King George V photographed in June
1918 along with Charlotte, a long-lived
royal parrot. The tent appears to be
that used by Queen Victoria for her
Jubilee garden parties.

Buckingham Palace + garden

Four photographs of the garden taken by King George V's third son, Henry, Duke of Gloucester, on 10 February 1914, from Queen Mary's photograph album. The boathouse, open to the water, is visible in the top right-hand photograph.

The King had a strict daily routine, inspired by his naval training; he would check the barometer and his red boxes, have breakfast, read *The Times*, write up his diary, work with his private secretary, perhaps hold a reception, then disappear for a brisk walk of a measured mile around the garden before lunch at 1.30 p.m. sharp. He would rest for quarter of an hour, fulfil his afternoon engagements and then have a game of tennis to relax before whatever the evening might bring. He had an indoor court in one of the conservatories but soon installed one of the all-weather En-Tout-Cas outdoor courts – as used by all the keenest and best players, and costing about £175 – on the site of the present tennis court.

To celebrate their twentieth wedding anniversary in 1913 the King and Queen planted a London plane tree opposite their private apartments. The Queen was in the garden as often as her busy life allowed, for she was always interested and had very definite likes and dislikes – she liked especially spring flowers and blossom trees and she had a hatred of ivy, which the gardeners learned to respect. The garden, with freshly flowering beds of hyacinths and primulas, or a romantic view across the lake, makes regular appearances in the large, red-leather-bound photograph albums in which she recorded her life. Visitors were almost always ushered outside to be photographed, and these informal pictures sit easily beside the grander images of state occasions.

The primulas and hyacinths merge with photographs of the endless farewells to the Guards' battalions leaving for war in the late summer and autumn of 1914: three members of their Household were amongst the first to be killed. The King's visits to the battlefields and dressing stations for the wounded in France and his daily letters to the Queen meant that they knew far more of the realities of war than most of the British people. They stayed in London for long periods, they offered the Palace for a hospital but it was thought 'too inconvenient' and the Queen worked at an endless round of comforting and encouraging – at war relief charities, cheering the workers in soup kitchens and factories, visiting hospitals and sympathising with bereaved relatives. Convalescing officers spent their summer afternoons in the Palace garden, ferried to and fro in carriages from the Royal Mews, and there were garden teas ('parties' seeming no longer the right word) for the wounded and the brave. On a rare quiet afternoon Queen Mary sat writing letters in the small tent on the lawn where she and the King liked to work outdoors, as Queen Victoria had once done: 'Since several days the weather has become warm & delicious', she wrote in May 1915, 'the

Queen Mary and the Landworkers' Parade in the courtyard of Buckingham Palace, 19 March 1918.

flowers & lilacs are coming out & the freshness of everything is really beautiful, one could be happy <u>if</u> only this terrible load of anxiety did not exist.'[41] She was writing to her 93-year-old aunt, Princess Augusta of Cambridge, Dowager Grand Duchess of Mecklenburg-Strelitz, and so 'this terrible load of anxiety' was a euphemism for a family, as well as for countries, at war.

In those later war summers, the dreadful summer of the Somme, 1916, and the hardly less terrible year afterwards, it was a much recorded phenomenon of English life that gardens and the countryside appeared ever more beguilingly beautiful, as if in defiance of the vileness of war. At Buckingham Palace, in the cool shade of the trees, with the sunlight sparkling on the lake, this was certainly so: because of the war, more 'ordinary' people than ever before had seen these gardens for the first time, but the officers and men who were helped to their chairs or limped around the lake had paid an inordinate price for their privilege. From the King's and Queen's points of view, it was the least they could do.

One day in the summer of 1918 the Queen, having toured allotments around London and been photographed with a piglet and rabbits, ever smiling through the cabbages, came straight home and photographed the Palace's war effort vegetable plots. Cabbages were appearing in the garden for the first time since the days of the Duke of Buckingham.

After the Armistice the garden parties were resumed, at first as expressions of gratitude to the armed forces and the nurses, and in 1920 a particular party was given for holders of the Victoria Cross. Gradually the royal regime was resumed and the King and Queen were less at the Palace: but through the 1920s and into the 1930s the summer season was celebrated whatever the ups and downs of the world outside the garden walls. In her down-to-earth way Queen Mary always referred to the regular arrival of 'our garden party', making it sound as though the advent of a few thousand people on the lawn was no more than a cosy vicarage tea-party.

King George V and Queen Mary celebrated their Silver Jubilee on 6 May 1935, a fine day of cheering crowds, a service in St Paul's, and appearances on the Palace balcony before and after lunch. In the afternoon they sat in their garden reading letters and answering telegrams of congratulation.

ABOVE AND RIGHT Garden produce from the 'digging for victory' effort during the First World War; Queen Mary had been visiting allotments around London in July 1918 and clearly decided that the home-grown efforts should be recorded (detail).

The garden at Buckingham Palace has a public as well as a private rôle to fulfil. Bedding plants need to be weeded with meticulous neatness, and a ready supply of young plants kept on hand in the gardeners' yard (below) to make good any specimens that fail to thrive.

After dinner it was out onto the balcony again: 'The greatest number of people in the streets I have ever seen in my life', the King noted in his diary. The crowds accompanied them on tours around London: 'I'd no idea they felt like that about me,' he was heard to remark. 'I am beginning to think they must really like me for myself.'[42] Just over eight months later, on Monday 20 January 1936, he died at Sandringham, with his beloved May by his side.

~

What of King Edward VIII, the eleven-months' King? He did not hurry his broken-hearted mother out of the Palace; she took leave of her lovely rooms 'with a sad heart' in July, and on 1 October noted 'My last day in dear Buckingham Palace.'[43]

Edward had moved into the Palace with his parents in 1910 when he was 16 (there is still a Norway maple 'Schwedleri' with his name on the plaque growing in the Palace garden; as Prince of Wales he had originally planted one in 1913 but it had to be replaced in 1929), and he and his younger brother Bertie had strained to get away from what they felt was 'the gilded prison'.[44] As the glamorous, golden and popular Prince of Wales, Prince Edward had lived at York House, St James's Palace, but had made his real home at Fort Belvedere at the southern extremity of Windsor Great Park, the only place where he said he felt truly happy. At the Fort he was an enthusiastic gardener, wielding a machete to beat down the overgrown rhododendrons, then planting many more of the beautiful Himalayan hybrids. He had seriously knowledgeable friends in Eric Savill – who became Sir Eric and the Deputy Ranger of the Great Park in 1937 and was the maker of the Savill Garden at Windsor – and the greatest rhododendronophile of them all, Lionel de Rothschild of Exbury in Hampshire, who was president of the Rhododendron Association, of which the Prince became patron.

One of King Edward VIII's first acts as sovereign was to fly from Sandringham to London. The first King to travel by air, he meant to become a thoroughly modern monarch. He didn't want to live in Buckingham Palace (he had no love for Windsor Castle, Balmoral or Sandringham either and instituted strict economies at all three) – which he regarded as 'enemy territory'; Clive Wigram (one of the enemy, who was a private secretary to King George V) said to John Reith of the BBC that if the King did not live at the Palace 'that would be the beginning of the end of the British Empire, as Buckingham Palace was the centre of it'.[45]

During his one brief summer the King did use the Palace for the round of receptions and parties, which he accomplished with an effortless charm, according to those who were prepared to give him the benefit of the doubt. Like most keen gardeners, he talked of his own, and was proud of his old-fashioned and 'outspokenly suburban' rock garden[46] at the Fort, as well as of his rhododendrons. He did veto plans for a stony memorial to his father and suggest the money be spent on the George V Playing Fields scheme, which became a nationwide blessing. For a while he honestly thought he could be King as well as have his private life at the Fort, with his golf and gardening, dancing to the gramophone, his swimming and dining parties, and Wallis Simpson. When it became clear that this was not possible, in December, he abdicated and 1936 became 'the year of three kings'.

Edward's younger brother, who became King George VI, was also a keen gardener, with his own passion for rhododendrons and azaleas, which he had planted at Royal Lodge, Windsor. Taming the rhododendron jungle there had given an outlet for his energies after he gave up hunting in the early 1930s, selling his horses as a token response to the harsh economic circumstances of the Depression years. Also he had married a gardener from a family of gardeners, Lady Elizabeth Bowes-Lyon. Lady Elizabeth had been brought up with 'a sense of good taste and a love of plants and animals' inherited from her mother, Lady Strathmore, and particularly shared with her younger brother David.[47] The long Bowes-Lyon family association with the Royal Horticultural Society was continued when David Bowes-Lyon (1902–61) began his lifelong commitment to the society in the 1930s. He inherited the hauntingly beautiful eighteenth-century garden of St Paul's Waldenbury in Hertfordshire, where he and his sister, now Queen Elizabeth, had spent much of their childhood.

Queen Mary at the garden party for holders of the Victoria Cross, 26 June 1920.

Sir David (he was knighted in 1959) was always a stalwart of the horticultural establishment and became president of the RHS and a member of the joint committee with the National Trust that pioneered the rescue and conservation of fine gardens for the nation after the Second World War – the garden of Hidcote Manor in Gloucestershire was the first they saved.

For his sister, Queen Elizabeth, there was only ceremonial gardening at a distance. She became royal patron of the RHS (as did the King), smiling through the annual tour of the rock gardens (the photographs always seemed to be of rock gardens) at the Chelsea Flower Shows, planting many trees with silver spades that would never be used again, and accepting innumerable bouquets of the flowers she so clearly delighted in, but it was not the hands-on gardening that she would have loved. Of all kings and queens, King George VI and Queen Elizabeth were to have the hardest time at Buckingham Palace, and yet from many accounts the Queen's sunny determination and vivacity made it a happy place. At quiet times the 'little Princesses' Elizabeth and Margaret rode round the garden on their bicycles (Princess Elizabeth remarking that 'people here need bicycles' *inside* the Palace), feeding the ducks or boating (it was Princess Elizabeth who fell into the lake) or busily working at nature projects with the Palace Girl Guide troop, with 'Brownie' Princess Margaret tagging along. Far from the 'Peter Pan' image of *Punch*'s Coronation Cartoon of 28 April 1937, the Princesses dutifully fed the fish daily with *Daphnia* (water-fleas) delivered in frozen portions by the 'fleaman'.[48] The King loved to play tennis vigorously every day, and Queen Elizabeth brought a 1930s glamour to the garden with her long, floating dresses, tip-tilted hats and parasols. The abiding images of their short pre-war summers are the 'Faerie Queen' portraits that Cecil Beaton was summoned to take one fine and fairly breezy morning in the

ABOVE Queen Elizabeth at Kew Gardens, 6 November 1990.

FAR LEFT Emily Sartain (1903–90), *Rhododendron williamsianum* decoration in watercolour for King George VI's signature as patron of the Royal Horticultural Society, 1936.

LEFT Emily Sartain, Magnolia, lilac and rose decoration in watercolour for Queen Elizabeth's signature as patron of the Royal Horticultural Society, 1937.

ABOVE The corgis are walked daily in the garden when The Queen is in residence – a familiar sight to the policemen on duty in the garden's police sentry box, set on the corner of the lawn beside the North Conservatory. Behind the sentry box can be seen a curving avenue of Indian horse chestnuts, *Aesculus indica*, planted in 1961.

BELOW Here the corgis' exercise, with a footman in summer uniform, coincides with preparations for the garden parties, including washing the lanterns on the terrace.

3

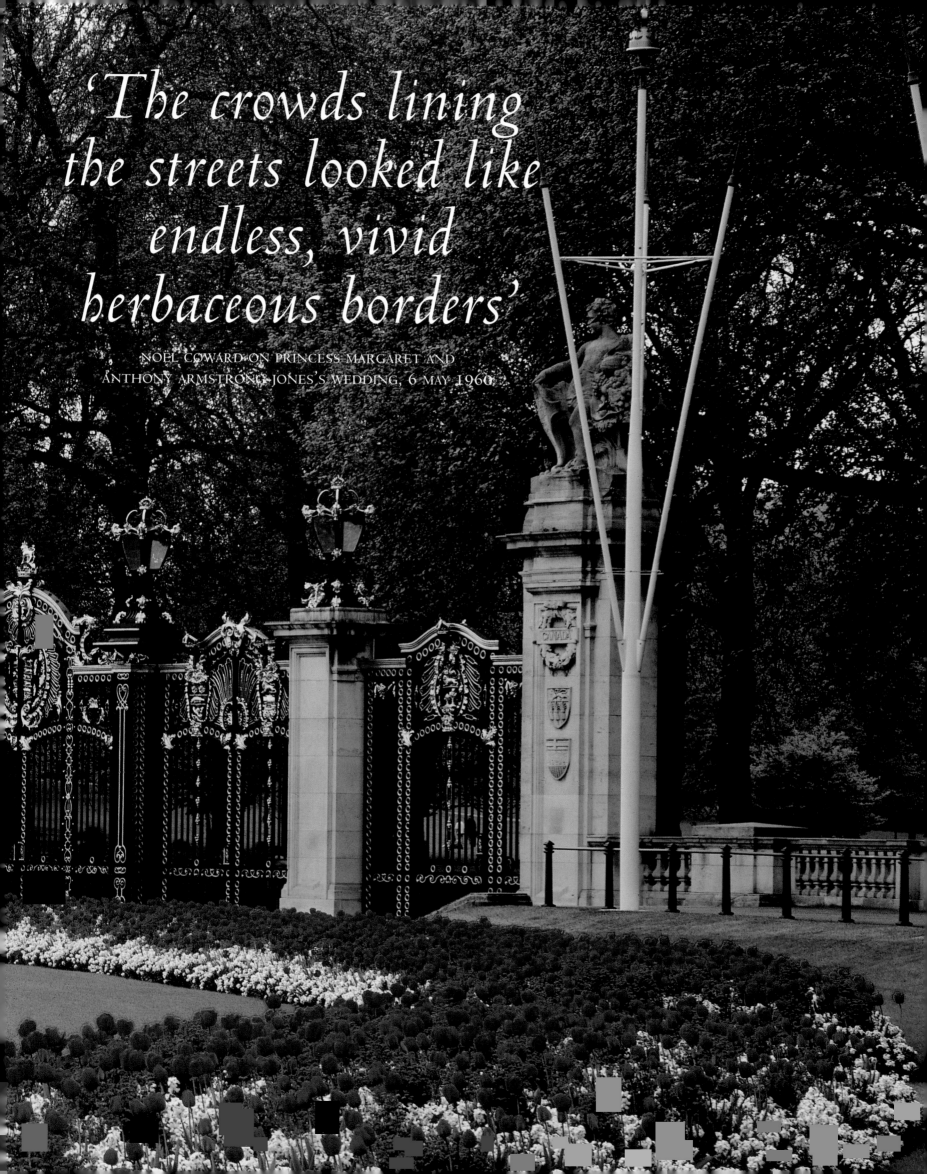

'The crowds lining the streets looked like endless, vivid herbaceous borders'

NOËL COWARD ON PRINCESS MARGARET AND
ANTHONY ARMSTRONG-JONES'S WEDDING, 6 MAY 1960

3
THE HOUSE AT THE TOP OF THE MALL
The front garden

The Queen's Gardens, around the Victoria Memorial, with the gates into Green Park. A bold display in the beds encircling the *rond point* planted by the gardeners of St James's Park, with distinctly regal overtones in the colour scheme of red, deep blue and gold.

IT WAS WITH A CERTAIN CRISPNESS that Queen Anne had informed her old admirer the Duke of Buckingham that though his house now faced The Mall, this was not to be used as his front drive. Naturally his coach would need to enter St James's Park on leaving his front gates, but it could go 'only from his house through St James's Mews passage [Stable Yard] into St James's Street and no otherwise'. The privileges of the Park were carefully guarded; there were to be only coaches with the royal arms, no horse riders and, since Londoners had become accustomed to walk there since the days of Charles I, they were not allowed to wear pattens (wooden overshoes), walk on the grass or carry 'burthens', and there were to be no dogs, no beggars and no sellers of anything. The only person allowed to ride, apart from the Queen's guards, was Henry Wise, the Deputy Ranger and Royal Gardener.[1]

Wise had inherited a park in a neglected state: one storm in 1703 had uprooted a hundred elm trees. He left it much improved. He was an expert at moving large trees and he had planted some 350 limes, widened the canal and repaired the sluice system to keep the water fresh and flowing. It was Wise's Park that became a great parade ground for the *beau monde*. The Duke and Duchess of Buckingham had a spectacular prospect from their front windows:

> The Mall was the most fashionable part, and there the Silvias, Clarindas, Belindas and Elviras of the *Tatlers* and *Spectators* swept along patched and painted, hooped and farthingaled *à outrance*, adorned with fly-caps, top-knots, and commodes, tightlaced bodies, laced aprons, and flounced petticoats, for the display of which the gown was gathered in folds behind. There the Philanders and Strephons, and the rest of the 'pretty fellows' flirted with those belles whom they rivalled in extravagant absurdity of dress and modish affectation. Decked out in square-tailed silk or velvet coats of all the colours of the rainbow, they tripped mincingly along upon their toes humming a tune, with a small hat on the top of a wheelbarrowful of periwig, covered with a bushel of powder.

These 'periwig planters' finished off their ensembles 'with pearl-coloured stockings, shoes with red heels and no doubt noses to match the heels, for those were glorious times ... The days and nights of four-bottle men.'[2]

It was partly the simple changing of dinner time from 5 in the afternoon to 8 or 9, with no time left for an evening promenade, that brought duller times to the Park. The milkmaids who sold 'sillabub' – fresh, still-warm frothy milk topped with Spanish wine – had become 'insolent milkwomen'. Rosamund's Pond and the duck decoy ponds were filled in because of the 'stinking exhalations' of those waters, according to the complaints of the residents near Buckingham Gate, and in winter

'The Crush in The Mall with Buckingham House in the Background', originally used as the frontispiece to Alexander Pope's *Man of Taste* and taken from Jacob Larwood's *The Story of the London Parks* (1872).

Plan of St James's Park, Office of Works, 1710. This shows clearly the design for the vistas, radiating from Horse Guards Parade on the right, with The Mall ending on the Duke of Buckingham's house. The gardens of St James's Palace are at centre right, with Pall Mall and St James's Square beyond.

After Paul Sandby (1725–1809). *A view of the late Encampment in St James's Park*, etching, 1780. RCIN 702576

P. Sandby R.A.Pinx.   James Fittler Sculp.

Unknown artist (published by G. Humphrey), *A Correct Representation of the Company going to and returning from His Majesty's Drawing Room at Buckingham Palace, St James's Park. A distant view of the Green Park*, hand-coloured etching with aquatint, 1822. The great houses of London can be seen ranged along Piccadilly in the background. RCIN 750804

the hundreds of spectators who cheered on the racing skaters on the canal were accused of 'whooping' their way through Sunday services at the Chapel Royal 'in view and hearing of the royal family'. In 1773 the Bow Street Justices announced their intention to arrest the disorderly 'till St James's Park and its environs be brought into that state of decorum that his Majesty's subjects may enjoy the privilege of walking and passing through that delightful spot without nuisance or interruption'. Seven summers later, when the Gordon Riots brought a looting mob to the City, the militia regiments were camped out in the Park and George III went out to visit them almost every day.[3]

That accident of design from 1660, when André Mollet's *patte d'oie* vista of The Mall had pointed fatefully at Arlington House, had by the 1770s come almost full circle: the Queen's House, soon to be Buckingham Palace, was now embraced into St James's Park. The Thomas Wright proposal of 1766 (see page 56) for a new palace in the Park revealed the thinking that united them. In the 1820s Frederick Trench proposed a ceremonial route to St Paul's Cathedral from Soane's fantasy palace in Hyde Park;[4] what came to pass was that George IV and John Nash's architectural progress from Regent's Park to Piccadilly and along The Mall (after Carlton House was demolished in 1827) ended at Buckingham Palace. All the criticisms of the costs and inadequacies of Nash's Palace were brought to nought by the alliance of events and landscape design. The Palace's future was assured by that yardstick of status, simply its location.

So, was the Palace to have St James's Park as a front garden? In a sense, and certainly visually, it seemed so. The trees of the Park ended in an open lawn outside the forecourt gates, and on the days when Queen Charlotte and subsequently George IV held 'drawing rooms' – the forerunners of presentation parties – the space was crowded with coaches and liveried footmen, and with an expectant, chattering company in their finest gowns and uniforms. The Mall was more like a garden drive than a ceremonial route, and for Queen Victoria's Coronation, on 28 June 1838, the Gold State Coach, drawn by eight cream horses with liveried walking grooms and the Yeomen of

John Rocque, *An Exact Survey of the City's* [sic] *of London, Westminster etc.*, 1746. Detail of St James's Park and Buckingham House.

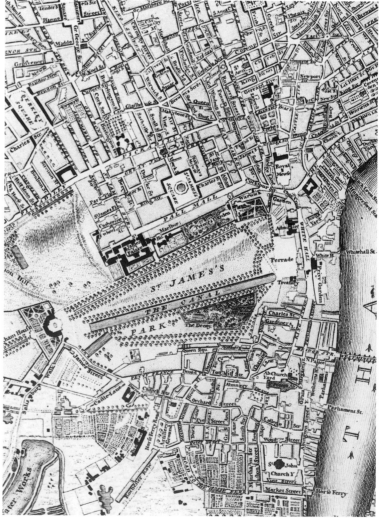

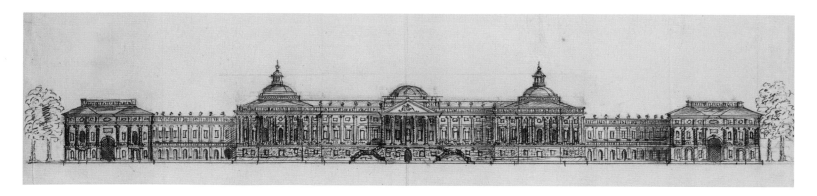

Thomas Wright (1711–86). *Elevation of proposed royal palace to be built in St James's Park*, pen and ink, 1766 (RL 17625a, detail). See page 56 for Wright's overall plan.

the Guard, wheeled left and along Constitution Hill to Piccadilly, down St James's Street to Pall Mall, Charing Cross and Whitehall to Westminster Abbey. She was amazed how 'the whole population seemed to have poured out in the direction of the Parks'.[5] In contrast, her wedding to Prince Albert on a rainy day in February 1840 took place at the Chapel Royal after a short carriage drive under the trees of The Mall. The Constitution Hill route was so predictable for public occasions that three attempts on the Queen's life were made there from amongst the trees: in June 1840, May 1842 and May 1849. In the spring of the previous year, 1848, there was great alarm about a Chartist rally planned for Trafalgar Square. The Queen was very nervous – some young supporters were breaking the lamps at her gates and shouting 'Vive la republique!' (on being arrested they burst into tears). She and Prince Albert took calming walks in the garden, and then were spirited away to Osborne.

The Queen agreed to sell the Royal Pavilion at Brighton and use the money for alterations at the Palace, and consequently Edward Blore's new east front was completed in 1847, with a balcony in the centre, facing out over the forecourt. This balcony was to be used for the first time on 1 May 1851, 'one of the greatest and most glorious days of our lives', as Victoria noted in her Journal, 'with which, to my pride & joy the name of my dearly beloved Albert is forever associated!' The day marked the opening of the Great Exhibition – the 'Peace Festival' – in Hyde Park, and so naturally they set out up Constitution Hill:

> At ½ p. 11, the whole procession in 9 state carriages was set in motion. Vicky and Bertie were in our carriage. Vicky was dressed in lace over white satin, with a small wreath of pink wild roses, in her hair … Bertie was in full Highland dress … .
> The Park presented a wonderful spectacle, crowds streaming through it – carriages and troops passing, quite like the Coronation Day, and for me, the same anxiety.

However, all went well, the Queen declared the Exhibition open – 'uniting the industry and art of all nations of the earth' – they looked around the Crystal Palace, and then returned to their own: 'We reached the Palace at 20 m. past 1 and went out on the balcony, being loudly cheered.'[6]

Part of the preparatory planning for this great day had included a formal water garden for the space between the Palace and The Mall, submitted at Prince Albert's request by William Andrews Nesfield (1793–1881) in 1849. Nesfield had had a colourful career, serving with Wellington in the Peninsular campaign and retiring to become a successful watercolourist, then giving that up for landscape gardening; in his letter of proposal he signed himself as a 'landscape architect', an early use of that professional title. The architectural gardens were 'proposed to occupy portions of St James's and the Green Parks east of and contiguous to Buckingham Palace', and their design flamboyantly demonstrated Nesfield's speciality of scroll patterns, *broderie* in box hedges and coloured gravels. The gardens were to stand right and left of the principal route through the centre to The Mall, two large parterres aligning with two canals with fountains. Nesfield wrote that 'the most requisite features … however are Fountains, which should be on the largest scale admissible in order to avoid the common place character so frequently observed in public and private gardens'. To create national interest he suggested sculptures representing the navy and army, and additional statues of the kings and queens of England. The south, or Queen's, garden was to have Victoria's initials in box with further box scrolls on a background of Derbyshire spar chippings, pounded red brick and Kensington gravels. The Prince's north parterre was complementary. The trees were to be limes; cedars

OPPOSITE The Wellington Arch at Hyde Park Corner defines the north-west corner of the garden. It was originally crowned with an immense statue of the Duke of Wellington on horseback. This was replaced by the present sculpture, *The Quadriga of Peace*, showing Peace descending onto a Roman war chariot, by Adrian Jones (1845–1938). The *Quadriga* was exhibited at the Royal Academy in 1891, admired by the Prince of Wales, later King Edward VII, and eventually raised to its lofty position in 1912.

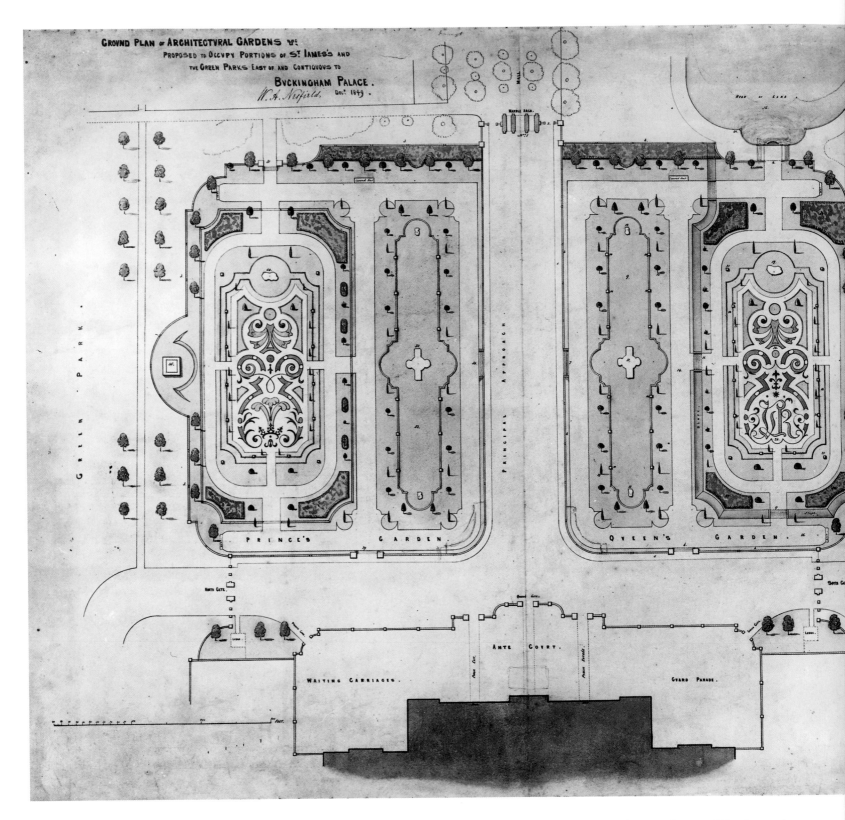

William Andrews Nesfield (1793–1881), *Ground Plan of Architectural Gardens to occupy portions of St James's and the Green Parks east and contiguous to Buckingham Palace*, pen and coloured washes, 1849. The 'Queen's Garden' is on the right, the 'Prince's Garden' on the left.

of Lebanon would be more desirable but they would not thrive in the London air. The fountains were to be monumental – the Queen's was '35 ft [10.7 metres] high to represent Britannia on the apex of a rock directing Plenty to diffuse her gifts over the Globe, which rests on the shoulders of Atlas, attended by Commerce and Neptune'. The Prince's was St George and the Dragon on a rock surrounded by Father Thames and Fame and Victory. The final touch to each garden was a 70-foot (21.3-metre) obelisk surmounted by a 'burnished gilt ball' to provide perspective from the Park, and engraved with the names of naval and land victories.[7]

Nesfield was fulfilling his brief from Prince Albert for a garden to outshine anything in Europe in homage to the monarch and her nation, but in this instance the monarch did not agree. She definitely preferred to see the groves of trees in the Park from her windows,[8] so the scheme was vetoed.

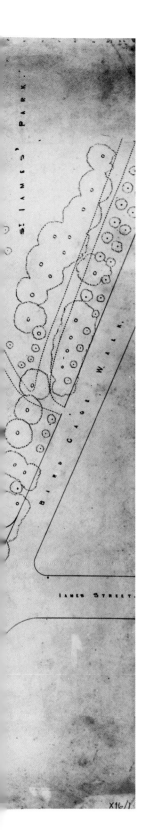

Being honored by the commands of
His Royal Highness Prince Albert, to prepare
Designs for the arrangement and decoration of
the ground East of Buckingham Palace,
the following propositions and observations
are respectfully submitted for the consideration
of His Royal Highness, and their Lordships
the Commissioners for the improvements of
Buckingham Palace.

By,
their Obedient Humble Servant
William. A. Nesfield,
Eton 31 Dec.r 1849   Landscape Architect &c

With reference to the accompanying Designs,
the primary object has been to appropriate
every portion of ground which can be commanded
between the Palace and Stafford House.
    Among all the celebrated examples on
the Continent, it will be found that
magnitude has hitherto been the great aim,
and although the space which is now,

LEFT William Andrews Nesfield, letter of submission
to HRH the Prince Consort and Commissioners for
the Improvement of Buckingham Palace.

BELOW William Andrews Nesfield, *Isometrical Sketch* of a
*Fountain Compartment: the Prince's Fountain with St George
and the Dragon, Father Thames and Fame and Victory*, pen
and watercolour, 1849.

BELOW AND RIGHT Queen Victoria's Diamond Jubilee, June 1897. The official photographs show the procession leaving the Palace to drive up Constitution Hill on the long route to Westminster Abbey, via Piccadilly, Trafalgar Square and Whitehall. On the right the procession returns via The Mall.

Nesfield was bitterly disappointed – he had refused other commissions and staked his future on this grandiose brief; the Prince was sympathetic though, and through his influence Nesfield designed the setting for Decimus Burton's Palm House at Kew, including the Pagoda and Broad Walks and the Syon Vista; and he made the formal gardens for the Horticultural Society in Kensington, the scene of Prince Albert's ill-fated last tree-planting, before his death in December 1861. If Prince Albert had lived, undoubtedly the arts of garden and landscape design would have benefited from his further championship and perhaps the garden of Buckingham Palace would have become a very different place.

The balcony was not just for celebrations: at the start of the Crimean War on 24 February 1854, the Queen wrote to her Uncle Leopold: 'The last battalion of the Guards (Scots Fusiliers) embarked to-day. They passed through the courtyard here at seven o'clock this morning. We stood on the balcony to see them – the morning fine, the sun rising over the towers of old Westminster Abbey – and an immense crowd collected to see these fine men, and cheering them immensely … a touching and beautiful sight.'[9] A year later war veterans were entertained in the garden. The war lasted two years, with 60,000 British casualties. Just under four years later, on a cold January day in 1858, the Princess Royal and Prince Frederick William of Prussia stepped through the now-celebrated window onto the balcony above the cheering crowds, after their wedding. Their son, born a year later, became Emperor Wilhelm II ('Kaiser Bill').

During the Queen's long absences from London the balcony and the blank, blinded windows must have looked sadly bereft. But the famous balcony and instantly recognisable façade were not to be neglected for ever. For sheer enchantment the wedding of Queen Victoria's grandson, the Duke of York, to Princess May of Teck on 6 July 1893 outshone all other occasions: 'not a hitch from first to last, not an if or a but!!', wrote Lady Geraldine Somerset:

> it was the *most heavenly* day ever *could* be – such a summer's day as you get solely and only in England … the *most brilliant* glorious *really* tropical sunshine with tropical heat, – yet with it mercifully air from time to time refreshed one and recovered one! … the town was alive!! swarms everywhere! … Piccadilly was beautifully decorated; but anything to equal the loveliness of St James's Street I never saw – it was like a bower from end to end … garlands of green across and across between the Venetian masts with bracelets of flowers suspended from them, *too pretty.*[10]

The bride was in a simple dress of white and silver, her small lace veil fastened with a diamond rose of York; she acknowledged the applause with her 'sideways smile'[11] and with a little nervous wave of her white-gloved hand. When all was done, the Queen wrote in her Journal: 'We drove back amidst the same tremendous cheering. Mary [the bride's mother] had been a little upset, but was very brave. We got home before everyone else. The heat was very great, quite overwhelming. Went to the middle room, with the balcony, overlooking the Mall, and stepped out amidst much cheering. Very soon the Bride and Bridegroom arrived and I stepped out on the balcony with them, taking her by the hand, which produced another great outburst of cheering.'[12]

After the Queen's death at Osborne in 1901 there were discussions about her memorial. The Committee for the Queen's Memorial proposed putting a statue under a canopy in front of the Palace and removing the central line of trees of The Mall to make a wide carriageway leading to a distant arch, where The Mall met Trafalgar Square. The new Queen Alexandra was a keen photographer[13] and she recorded the scene so soon to be changed; two pages of her album for the 1890s and early 1900s in the Royal Photograph Collection are covered with almost time-lapsed snapshots of the forecourt; a carriage approaching through the narrow central avenue of The Mall, the gates being opened, a courtier walking across the forecourt, soldiers manoeuvring into their place.

Plans for the Memorial were open to a limited design competition in early 1901. Five architects, representing England, Scotland and Wales, had six months to submit their schemes. The preferred design was by Aston Webb, the son of an engraver and artist from Clapham, who had already built the Cromwell Road front of the Victoria and Albert Museum (for which Queen Victoria had laid the foundation stone in 1899), thus completing the Prince Consort's visionary South Kensington cultural centre 'Albertopolis', which included all the museums and the Albert Hall. Aston Webb's scheme for the front of Buckingham Palace was equally staggering in scale: the

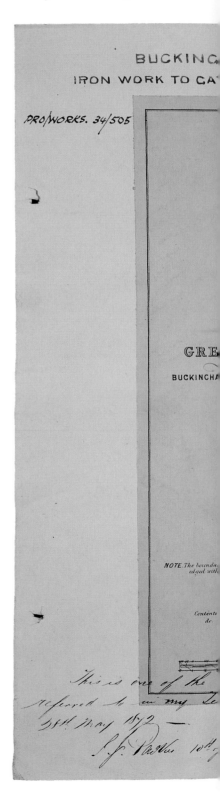

General plan for the works to the gates and boundary wall of the garden in 1850. The letters A, B, C, D, E and F refer to the construction of the present Hyde Park Corner, Grosvenor Place and Buckingham Palace Road gates.

forecourt railings were to be extended and elaborated by arches and colonnades from which sprang a colonnaded *rond point*, cutting an enormous semi-circular mouthful out of Green Park, The Mall and St James's Park, and dwarfing the focal statue of Queen Victoria. The architectural concept was that the Memorial embraced the whole Mall, with the Admiralty Arch (as it was called because it provided naval office space and an apartment for the First Lord of the Admiralty) screening the commercial developments of Northumberland Avenue and the Strand. It is worth adding that Thomas Graham Jackson's runner-up scheme was even more monumental, carving an enormous colonnaded square out of the parks and filling it with Italianate gardens and fountains around a memorial statue. The dramatic architectural perspectives give the impression of London being transformed by a Parisian or Berlin scale of city planning, but the context also has to be recalled: this was 1901, the high noon of the British Empire, with no thought of thirteen years hence. The whole of London's West End,

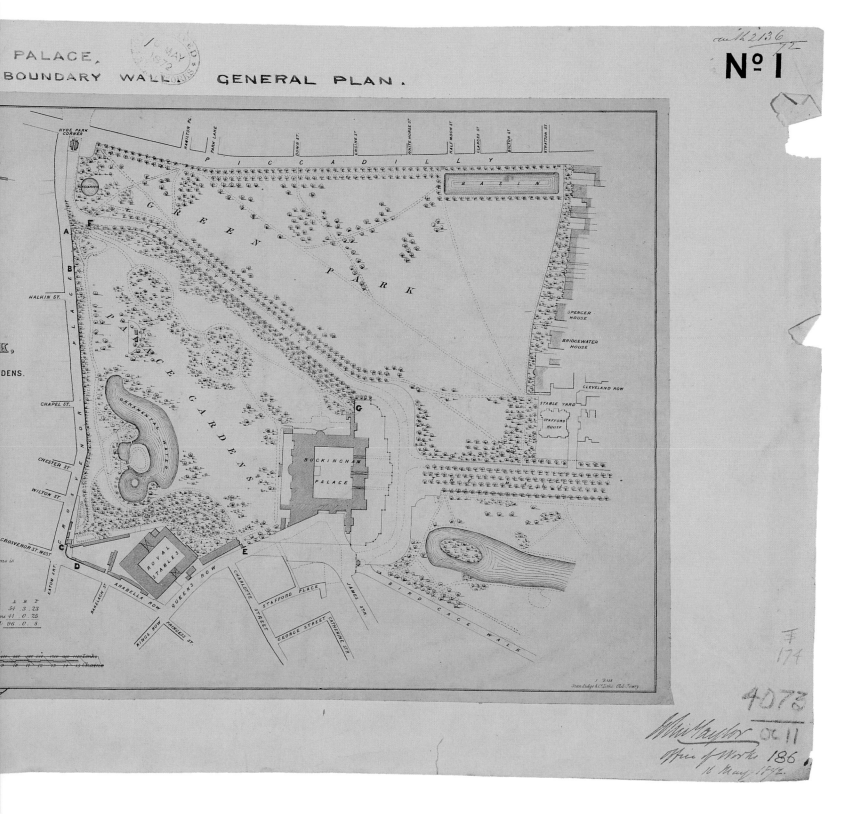

One of Queen Alexandra's photographs of the forecourt, from a series taken before the works for the Victoria Memorial were started. This shows the south centre gate, c.1902 (detail).

OPPOSITE Beatrice Emma Parsons (1870–1955), *Irises. Buckingham Palace from St James's Park*, watercolour. RCIN 452861

thanks to the possibilities opened up by steel-framed building construction, was being rebuilt in the grand manner and scale of the Edwardian baroque. Contemporary buildings included the Ritz Hotel across Green Park, the Piccadilly Hotel, clubs in Pall Mall, ministries in Whitehall, the Methodist Central Hall opposite Westminster Abbey and, generally acclaimed the most elegant of them all, John Burnet's King Edward VII Galleries in Montagu Place for the British Museum, on which work started in 1904.

A model of Aston Webb's memorial design was put on public display at St James's Palace, and the late Queen's vast family were all consulted. The artistically minded Princess Louise (1848–1939), patroness of the young Edwin Lutyens and friend of Gertrude Jekyll, disagreed, suggesting a site in Green Park for the statue 'because of her mother's love of being surrounded by flowers and trees, as well as her hatred of asphalt'.[14]

King Edward VII approved the scheme, though thankfully refused to allow the name of The Mall to be changed to 'The Processional Way', and public contributions to pay for the Memorial poured in. Aston Webb began work on the Admiralty Arch, though this was far from straightforward as their lordships at the Admiralty kept changing their minds, and the architect was working on the Royal Naval College at Dartmouth, Birmingham University and Imperial College in Kensington at the same time. The King knighted Webb in 1904; he was awarded the Royal Gold Medal for Architecture in 1907 and his memorial design, under the weighty title 'The Proposed Architectural Treatment of the Surroundings to the National Memorial to Queen Victoria in front of Buckingham Palace', won him election to the Royal Academy.

However, the front of Buckingham Palace could not be turned into a building site

Sir Aston Webb (1849–1930), the winning design in the competition for the setting of the Victoria Memorial, published in *The Builder*, 2 November 1901.

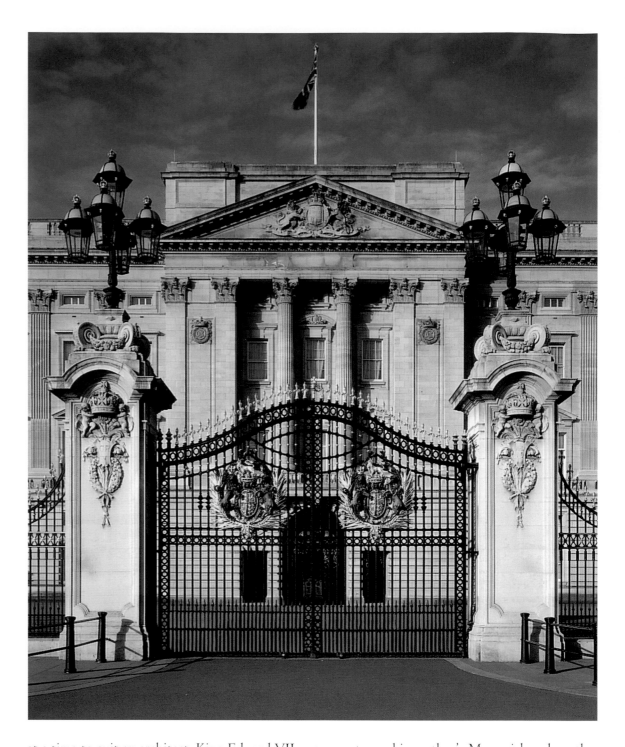

The Grand Entrance to Buckingham Palace, with the cipher of King George V and the date 1911.

at a time to suit an architect. King Edward VII was never to see his mother's Memorial, and another funeral and another coronation had to pass before work started. King George V, with his deep unwillingness to be seen as isolated from his people, gently sought to tone down the monumentality of the colonnades (which gave the flower beds around the *rond point* more prominence) and he would not have the style of gate piers and railings of the Palace forecourt significantly changed: the north central gate piers carry the cipher of Queen Victoria, the south central piers that of King Edward VII, and the main central piers commemorate the Coronation of 1911. (The stone piers are still as originally designed by Decimus Burton, but the gates with their heraldic trophies are Aston Webb's designs, made by the Bromsgrove Guild of Ironworkers.) These 'economies' pleased the Treasury, who found that the memorial funds would now stretch to the necessary refacing of Blore's east front of the Palace, where the Caen stone had weathered badly and was crumbling away. The work was done in thirteen weeks by the stonemasons and builders Leslie & Company, without disturbing the glass in the windows. The King gave five hundred workmen a thank-you dinner in October 1913.[15]

Queen Mary's album has a photograph of the brand-new Memorial taken on 1 November 1913. Queen Victoria (without a canopy) sits on her marble throne with a view, as she would surely have wished, of the trees in The Mall and the Park, with Truth, Justice and Motherhood as her companions. A gilded Victory flies above her. As Queen of a seafaring nation her throne is supported on galleons; bronze figures of Progress, Peace, Shipbuilding and War guard her; and mermaids, naiads and sea-gods gather around. The sculptor was Thomas Brock, who carved the Queen and her throne out of a single block of marble; King George V knighted him immediately after the unveiling.

On 10 February 1914, taking the King and Queen to the State Opening of Parliament, the carriage procession swept around the Memorial and down The Mall for the first time. On the following fine 22 June, for the Trooping of the Colour, the Memorial must have shone out in its pristine whiteness against the blue sky and scarlet uniforms. It is noticeable that, though the crowds were presumably streaming through the Park to The Mall, they must have been prevented from entering the *rond point*, for outside the Palace gates there were only a few sedate observers, with a small group of special guests standing on the Memorial's steps.

Queen Mary's diary and albums take up the story. Six days later there was the news of the assassination of Archduke Franz Ferdinand and his wife in Sarajevo – 'a great shock to us',[16] she wrote, recalling their happy visit to Windsor of the previous year. The King and Queen left for Windsor as usual, only to return to London in August, an unheard-of thing, as it became inevitable that Britain would be drawn into a European war. 'War news very grave' was the diary theme, and on 2 August: 'Walked with G. in the garden – After dinner a large crowd assembled in front of the Palace & sang "God Save the King" and we went on the balcony & had a very good reception – The Govt has not yet decided what our action is to be.'[17] The following evening, 3 August, they were called out onto the balcony, three times, and on 4 August: 'Fine. Awful day of suspense ... At 12. we sent an ultimatum to Germany & at 7 p.m. she declared war on us ... We went on to the balcony at 8 p.m. & again at 11.15 after the news of war having been declared was out.'[18]

The new Victoria Memorial. An aerial photograph of 1919, from Queen Mary's photograph album.

Even in the mood of jingoistic optimism with which the war started, the people needed their King: King George V, dreading what was to come, needed his people, and a bond and a tradition were forged on those summer evenings. A few days later, on 9 August, when the King and Queen came down to their front gate to bid farewell to the 2nd Battalion of the Grenadier Guards, the crowd were politely standing around the Memorial, again with special guests, perhaps relatives of the soldiers, on the steps. There was a stream of front-gate farewells throughout August and into September: on 11 September a colour party consisting of the diminutive Prince of Wales in his khaki uniform, surrounded by what must have been the tallest guardsmen they could find.[19]

As the four terrible years dragged on, the crowds continued to gather at the Palace when the news was particularly bad – they had waited quietly at the railings for news of King Edward VII's emergency appendicitis operation in 1902 – but now, with the vast Memorial and Queen's Gardens in place, they crossed the sea of asphalt and (one hopes) stepped over the red tulips or geraniums, and no one stopped them. If the front of Buckingham Palace had some symbolic importance before, this was now multiplied. The 'front garden' became – as in every town or village street in England – the meeting place with the outside world. On Armistice Day, 11 November 1918 – 'the greatest day in the world's history', Queen Mary wrote in her diary – a day of comings and goings, of balcony appearances from breakfast time until late in the evening, with a band in the forecourt playing patriotic and popular songs,[20] photographs show that the crowd had 'embraced' the Memorial and some of them were clambering over the Queen-Empress's accommodating frame.

Everyone in that crowd must have had their memories of the occasion, passed down to children and grandchildren, but it is rare that they come out into the open. One bright little 4-year-old girl was there, and when she was 16 she put her memories into words: 'I was taken to Buckingham Palace in a pram, the pram was squashed in two by the crowd. I sat on a man's shoulder. I remember seeing the royal family on the balcony, and thinking that Princess Mary was waving to me especially. I remember the streets lined with flags, when the man put me down mum asked me why I hadn't said thank-you and I replied "I have not been introduced".'[21]

And so it has continued down the years, the balcony spotlit in a thousand camera flashes presiding over a history of its own: the Victory March of 9 July 1919 with a saluting pavilion outside the front gate; The Mall as a complete sea of black umbrellas for the Duke and Duchess of York's return from Canada; the balcony call in black, court mourning for King George V; that for the wedding of Lady Alice Montagu-Douglas-Scott and Prince Henry of Gloucester; the appearance of Winston Churchill and the King and Queen for VE Day in May 1945; the wedding of Princess Elizabeth and Prince Philip of Greece two-and-a-half years later; the

OPPOSITE The Victoria Memorial today.

Armistice Day, 11 November 1918: the euphoric crowd climbing over the Memorial for the first time. Photograph from Queen Mary's album.

THE HOUSE AT THE TOP OF THE MALL 139

Armistice Day, 11 November 1918: faces in the crowd. Photograph
from Queen Mary's album.

magnificently crowded balcony for the Coronation in 1953 and Prince Charles and Lady Diana's wedding kiss in 1981. Good and bad news is 'posted' on the railings in a small black frame – the death of a king, the birth of a princess – in a personal message, albeit from a distinguished physician, that people would make a special journey to read and long remember reading. There have been many happy forecourt send-offs after royal weddings but the need for those poignant front-gate farewells had lapsed until the death of Diana, Princess of Wales, when The Queen led her family down to her front gate on the day of the funeral to say goodbye. Most recently, in June 2002, The Queen reviewed her Golden Jubilee celebratory procession from the steps of the Victoria Memorial, and the forecourt was the setting for the formal welcome to the President of the United States and Mrs Bush in November 2003.

This history of Buckingham Palace's 'front garden' is perpetuated in the ceremonial traditions of the Queen's Guard, the seven regiments of the Household Division that dominate this territory. Five of the regiments were in Charles II's army; the Grenadiers, the 1st Regiment of Footguards, were with him in exile; the Scots Guards were his father's bodyguard in Scotland; the Coldstream Guards were originally part of the New Model Army but came south to keep order in London at the Restoration. Of the mounted regiments, the Life Guards first saw action at the Battle of Maastricht in 1672 and the Blues and Royals now combine a regiment of horse raised by Cromwell, which became the Royal Horse Guards, and Charles II's Royal Dragoons. The Irish Guards were formed in 1900 by Queen Victoria, and the Welsh Guards by King George V in 1915.

When Charles II had St James's Park laid out with its *patte d'oie*, The Mall as a finger of fate pointing at what was then Arlington House, the emphasis was still on Whitehall Palace as the King's principal residence and the home of the court. In 1698 Whitehall Palace, except for Inigo Jones's Banqueting House, burned down and the court removed to St James's Palace. Despite Sir Christopher Wren's grand scheme for a new Whitehall Palace, with elaborate formal flower gardens to cover Horse

William Simpson (1823–99), *Return of the Guards from the Crimea*, watercolour and bodycolour, July 1856. RL 16792

Guards Parade and extend into the Park, it was never rebuilt. The Horse Guards kept their parade ground, and the Arch on Whitehall (with its focus reversed) continued to be guarded, now as the carriage entrance to St James's Palace. The Guards enforced the strict control on who was allowed to drive through the Arch, a privilege reserved for the royal family and a few owners of the prized Ivory Pass. Trafalgar Square was completed early in Queen Victoria's reign (1841) and Admiralty Arch built as part of the Victoria Memorial, but history dictates that Horse Guards' Arch is still the principal entrance to St James's Palace and Buckingham Palace. The ceremonial parades of the Household Division in their regular duties of the Changing of the Guard, from Wellington Barracks in Birdcage Walk to Buckingham Palace, to St James's Palace, and in the mounting of the Guard at Whitehall, perpetuate and confirm this history.[22]

Trooping the Colour, 23 June 1936. Watching King Edward VIII take the salute at the ceremony (left to right): Princess Alice, Countess of Athlone; the Duchess of Kent; Princess Margaret and Princess Elizabeth of York; Queen Mary; the Duchess of York; the Duchess of Gloucester; the Hon. George Lascelles; the Princess Royal; Lady Patricia Ramsay; Princess Marie Louise; Princess Helena Victoria; Lady Maud Carnegie; James, Master of Carnegie; Lord Carnegie; Arthur, Duke of Connaught; unidentified; Lord Louis Mountbatten and Lady Louis Mountbatten. The group are all dressed in mourning for King George V.

4

'*...a haven walled off from the rest of the metropolis for over a century...*'

DAVID McCLINTOCK AND ELINOR WILTSHIRE,
THE LONDON NATURALIST, 1999

4

THE GARDENERS' GARDEN
From the 1830s to the present day

The gardener's constant companions – wheelbarrow and border fork – standing sentinel in the Rose Garden.

JUDGING BY THE RIVAL EDITORIALS in the gardening press of the time, the 1830s do seem to have been the nadir of the garden. In an editorial on 14 October 1837 the *Gardeners' Gazette* attacked the standard of maintenance at both Kew Gardens and Buckingham Palace: Kew's fortunes and reputation had tumbled since the death of Sir Joseph Banks in 1820 and a government committee of inquiry confirmed this dire state, leading to the appointment in 1841 of Sir William Hooker (1785–1865) as first director and the acclaimed saviour of Kew. At the Palace the target was William Townsend Aiton for his employment of fewer than a dozen men who were 'anything but gardeners' – including a pensioned footman, 'an old soldier from the Fusileer Guards', an old sailor who 'can hardly see' and was 'totally unfit for business', an 'ignorant' 18-year-old and a 'nervous, timid, half silly fellow, who is merely a fit butt for the rest'.[1] The professionalism of gardening was at stake; it was perfectly usual for kindly sea-captains and generals to give employment to ex-servicemen – and what was William IV but a kindly sailor-king? – but the nineteenth century was forging the regimes of the legendary Victorian head gardeners as surely as industrial iron and steel. Gardening was an 'improving' profession, according to the all-pervasive voice of John Claudius Loudon and his *Encyclopaedia* of 1822, a profession of refinement and method that turned mischievous 12-year-old boys into respected journeymen of 18 (hence the scandal of the 'ignorant' 18-year-old) and found them their 'own' establishment as a head gardener by the time they were 30.

The furore that sent William Hooker to Kew brought George Wyness as head gardener to Buckingham Palace in 1840. But whereas almost every movement of Sir William has been chronicled, very little is known of Head Gardener Wyness, except that almost immediately he created Queen Victoria's 'much improved' garden. Wyness was to be in charge of the garden for thirty-two years; if he was about 30 when appointed, and he died after two years' retirement, on 18 June 1874, that would have given him a life of a respectable sixty-four years. His status as the fully fledged product of the rigorous training in a large 'establishment' is confirmed by the substantial villa, standing in its own plot, that was built for him next to the gardeners' yard in the south-west corner of the garden. This house, the fuel to heat it and 35 shillings a week wages, were in his contract. However, the professional gardeners' pride was in the complete spectrum of provisions, and 'establishment' meant the walled garden for vegetables and fruit, with all its attendant peach and vine houses; and glasshouses for flowers for the house, table and family weddings and funerals. Pleasure gardens and lawns were an adjunct to all this and George Wyness may have been just a little looked down on for having *only* the latter, leaving all the interesting work to the Royal Gardens at Windsor, which supplied fruit, vegetables and flowers to the Palace as necessary.[2]

But Buckingham Palace was Buckingham Palace and a source of pride as the Queen's garden. George Wyness must have been a known appointee, certainly with Aiton's approval, and

ABOVE The garden in 1855, during George Wyness's time as head gardener. See also the plans on page 75.

LEFT The Victorian tradition of summer bedding is still continued in the garden. Pink pelargoniums flourish on the sunny terrace outside The Queen's private apartments, while the Herbaceous Border can be glimpsed over the balustrade.

Green's Patent Lawn Mowers, including the *Silens Messor*, illustrated in an advertisement in *The Garden*, 25 March 1905.

may well have come from Windsor or Kew, but the critical difference was that he lived in his garden and was the cohesive force uniting the disparate voices that came from the Household, the architects and builders working on the palace, the Office of Woods and Forests and perhaps residually from Windsor and Kew. With Wyness the Palace garden won its independence, further enforced when Prince Albert brought it directly under the Household's control.

Wyness and his men completed the lake's excavations, cutting away the neck of land that made the island, finishing the Mound and making the paths to the new Pavilion. With good gardening and regular maintenance it all became pleasantly 'gardenesque': loads of gravel were brought in to suit the paths to the royal perambulators, the old Brown/Chambers perimeter path was cleared and weeded, and strolling made more interesting with Nash/Aiton diversions around two glades containing pat-terned beds of spring and summer flowers. Tulips and polyanthus were followed by a regal scheme of red pelargoniums, white marguerite daisies and royal blue lobelia, which became *de rigueur* for all Victorian London gardens. Prince Albert's enthusiasm for new inventions brought one of the earliest lawn mowers into the garden, a rotary cutter drawn by a pony wearing made-to-measure leather boots, possibly one with the desirable 42-inch blades made by Shanks & Sons 'which could tidy an area of two and a half acres [1 hectare] in seven hours' instead of calling for three days' cutting with scythes. By the early 1860s Thomas Green held the Royal Warrant for supplying cylinder mowers, pushed by hand, and in 1865 he introduced his patent *Silens Messor* ('Silent Reaper'), with its large grass-collecting box, proudly announcing his 'Special Appointment to Her Most Gracious Majesty The Queen'.[3]

A final sweep with the leaf-blower and the grass around the north-east American beds is ready for the garden parties. The plants include *Hydrangea arborescens* 'Annabelle', a cercis cultivar 'Forest Pansy', whose purple colour will turn red in autumn, and a buckeye, *Aesculus parviflora*.

A surviving plan of 1855 testifies to Wyness's achievement, showing a garden of liveliness and colour. There were circuits of pleasure across lawns – via evergreen-sheltered groves of circular and fan-shaped flower beds, a delicate sprinkling of specimen trees (cedar, Scotch fir, pines, the monkey puzzle) and shrubs (hollies, privet, box, the 'spotted' laurel *Aucuba japonica variegata* and pampas grass) to a seat by the lake. There were walks on the island, to the boat house, and lastly to the Pavilion amongst its romantic greenery on the Mound. There was an ice-house at the Palace end of the Mound, and a small additional mound had been made to protect the Queen from the prying eyes in the new Palace Hotel, built opposite the site of the present Queen's Gallery. It was a very 'Victorian' garden.

In 1872 George Wyness was succeeded by Edwin Humphreys and for part of the following year, the three months to 30 June 1873, the Household accounts detail the garden expenses. Humphreys was paid £22 15s. wages, about the same as Wyness – £91 a year – and his assistant, H.B. Heath, was paid at nearly half that rate. The rest of the gardeners are collectively described as 'labourers' and so were presumably still a motley collection, their wages totalling £148 16s. 6d. Despite the profession's pride, there was still a great deal of menial weeding, raking and barrowing to be done. The lawn-mowing pony cost £22 to feed with an extra £3 10s. for harness repairs and shoes – not his lawn boots but iron shoes (was he too lowly to be shod in the Royal Mews?) for outside excursions with the cart that was the garden's only transport. Supplies were brought in – unending deliveries of gravel for the paths (£34 12s.) and artificial manure (guano, in addition to the product of the Mews, £6 8s. 3d.). Plants costing £300 were purchased from Henry Bailey and some were also supplied by Veitch's Royal Nursery in the King's Road, Chelsea.

Many of the trees and some of the plantings of shrubs from the 19th century still survive in the garden, and certain walks have a distinctly Victorian atmosphere. Here a 'spotted' laurel grows beside another great 19th-century favourite, a rhododendron.

During that summer of 1873 the Shah of Persia and his entourage stayed at Buckingham Palace in the Queen's absence: the garden accounts note 'Extra Expenses' for the Shah's visit, including one of Thomas Green's spanking new lawn mowers, costing £20 15s.[4] The documentary evidence for this visit is sparse, but the colourful stories are many; for example, the Household officials were shocked to learn that four prize-fighters (strictly unauthorised visitors to the Palace) had been admitted to the garden and that boxing fights were staged on the lawn.[5] More lurid tales have persisted concerning the wild parties and the cooking of ceremonial feasts on the best carpets, but the worst scandal concerns the supposed execution of one of the Shah's party in a duel, the body being apparently buried in the garden.[6] It should be added that the gardeners have never found any sign of human remains.

Humphreys had Queen Victoria's confidence over the replanting of the sheltering belt of trees beside Constitution Hill, and though he was only head gardener for eleven years (he may have resigned because of illness) he kept up the standards of the garden, despite the Queen's long absences. William Robinson's new magazine *The Garden* (started in 1871) had a 'Christmas treat' for readers in 1873 with a glimpse of the Palace garden: a certain 'N.N.H' signed the article, in which he says he does not like the building at all, but finds the 'jardin anglais' is 'remarkably good' and a 'cause for national pride'. He has clearly seen (whether from a window of the Palace Hotel or from inside the garden is not stated) the 'turfy glades, shady walks, plantations of handsome flowering shrubs [and] park-like trees' and some of the elms dating from Lord Arlington's time. He concludes that 'the art of the gardener has, indeed, gone far in the gardens of Buckingham Palace to redeem the blunders and shortcomings of its architects'.[7]

John Richard Stirling became head gardener in 1882, and his splendid garden formed the backdrop for the Jubilees of 1887 and 1897, which will be celebrated in the next chapter. Like many of the best head gardeners he seems to have been difficult (he was a contemporary of Lord Sackville's black-bearded giant of a gardener at Knole in Kent, remembered by Vita Sackville-West as terrifyingly majestic, set apart from other men in his pride and his power).[8] When Queen Victoria died in 1901 the management of the garden was transferred to the Office of Works and lost its independence to the Superintendent of St James's Park. Stirling, quite justifiably after nineteen years of loyal personal service to his Queen, refused to work under that particular Superintendent (whose name was Brown) and, despite King Edward VII's request that he stay, at least to see the garden through the Coronation, he stubbornly refused and was pensioned off. It was a sad day for the garden. Officialdom took charge and though Head Gardener Osborne worked right through the King's reign and until 1912, no head gardener was again appointed until 1928.

Looking from the window of the State Dining Room across the lawn. The tree on the far right is the copper beech planted by King Edward VII and Queen Alexandra in 1902.

It is time to look at the lawn. The main lawn between the Palace terrace and the lake is almost 2 hectares (5 acres) and has been so for more than a hundred years; the garden-party tents are still set out much in the same way as decreed in a plan of 1900. The camomile (*Chamaemelum nobile*) in the lawn is legendary, causing much comment as it responds to the tread of garden-party guests; it is persistent, to say the least, first recorded in the area 'this side of Hyde Park' in 1666.[9]

So old a lawn of scented velvety green evokes exactly the iconic English lawn, eulogised in Oxbridge quadrangles and in lawn-mower advertisements since the high days of Empire, when tea on such a tree-shaded spot was the abiding fantasy of home. A century ago there was no more perfect place for this symbol than Buckingham Palace, and here, as in an increasing number of gardens across the land, it was the product of lawn-mower

Mima Nixon (*fl.*1894–1918),
Buckingham Palace from the Gardens,
watercolour and bodycolour, 1915.
RCIN 450887

technology and an individual owner's perfectionism – in this instance, that of King Edward VII. The race to create a power-driven mower began with steam models made by three companies, including the Royal Warrant Holders, Greens. These great puffing and clanking monsters weighed in at around 1½ tonnes. James Ransome of Ipswich saw the potential of petrol power and in 1902 his company introduced their first model – 'Forty-two inches wide, powered by a six-horsepower engine, and weighing several hundredweight, it was a juggernaut, a gleaming roaring beast of a machine, but delicate and amenable compared with its steam-powered rival.'[10] Imagine a fine morning on the terrace, the King and his friends in jovial mood, for the arch-rivals in petrol and steam had been summoned for a race across the lawn. The King declared Ransome's petrol-driven mower the winner; 'cricket's bearded colossus, W.G. Grace, ordered one for his London County Cricket Club' at Sydenham and declared that 'whenever the ground is soft you could get on it with a motor mower when it would be impossible for a horse machine to be used without harm to the ground', and so Ransome's fortune was made and gardeners used petrol mowers throughout the twentieth century. At Buckingham Palace, such was the enthusiasm that the lawn was completely remade, topped with soil from the excavations for the Victoria Memorial and reseeded, rolled and endlessly watered, the painstaking beginnings of a perfect sward. The camomile survived. A royal wager and a smattering of technological revolution had contributed to a legend – as Eleanour Sinclair Rohde wrote, 'those of us who live in the Old Country, and those of us whose lot is cast in the great dominions beyond the seas, are equally proud of the fact that in the "islands of the West" we have the greenest and the most beautiful grass in the world'.[11]

Head Gardener Alfred J. Cole was in post from 1928 until 1954, through an eventful period which fostered the gardener's philosophy of carrying on with the routine despite the happenings in

Lotte Günthart, botanical drawing of the rose 'Queen Elizabeth', a modern cluster-flowered bush rose of pure, delicate pink, named for Queen Elizabeth The Queen Mother, when she was Queen.

There are still miles of paths and drives in the garden, all of which need regular raking, weeding and regravelling.

the 'big house' and the outside world. Cole enjoyed the kindness and confidence of Queen Mary, working to her special instructions – and under her eagle eye – to remove every trace of the ivy she hated, particularly from the Mound and from the walls of the Royal Mews. The ivy was replaced with flowering shrubs which immediately lightened the atmosphere. The year 1936 must have been a strange one, beginning with the sadness of the King's death, the uncertainties of the new regime and gossip about King Edward VIII's passion for rhododendrons – would he turn the whole garden into another Exbury? One thing was sure, he did not lack imagination and would have made some great changes – but abdication was change enough, and King George VI and Queen Elizabeth brought a happiness tinged with relief to the working atmosphere of both Palace and garden. Three brief summers of glamour were encapsulated in the Cecil Beaton photographs of the Queen. Did the gardeners watch unseen (how could they resist?) as she posed by the Waterloo Vase, on the terrace steps, in the Rose Garden, under the trees, in her fairy-tale tulle garden-party gown and with her parasol, as the elegant photographer followed her around?

For Cole and his much-reduced garden staff the war must have brought particular difficulties. The bombs that fell during 1940–41 necessitated a constant exhausting round of clearing up and repairing, cutting and carting damaged trees, making safe and carrying on – and then nightly fire-watching as it started all over again. As well as tending a garden in the 'front line', they also had to cope with the special priorities of protecting the King and Queen – army lorries on the lawn, a garden busy with patrols and emergency drill-practice, not unlike all the other militarily 'requisitioned' great houses and gardens in England. But this was Buckingham Palace, and though the grass might be grown for hay, and vegetables were cultivated in the 'Dig for Victory' cause, there were still the Queen's favourite lilacs, sweet peas and roses to care for, delicate symbols of a determination to survive.

Four particular trees – Indian horse chestnuts (*Aesculus indica*) – remain from Cole's time, two planted on 2 December 1935 for King George V and Queen Mary's Silver Jubilee and two planted to mark King George VI and Queen Elizabeth's Coronation in 1937. This Indian chestnut, with its panicles of pink-flushed flowers, had been introduced from the Himalayas by Joseph Hooker, son of Sir William, in 1851 but rose steadily in the Royal Horticultural Society's favour in the 1930s (First Class Certificate awarded 1933) and has now become a Palace favourite; a curving avenue of them was planted in 1961 for the present Queen, to shelter the walk from the North Terrace into the garden.

King George VI and Queen Elizabeth left a real legacy to gardening in their inspiration for the creation of the Valley Gardens in Windsor Great Park after the war, and in their encouragement of the progress of the neighbouring Savill Garden. They also gave their support to the National Gardens Scheme, opening Sandringham garden for the Queen's Institute of District Nursing and the Gardeners' Royal Benevolent Fund charities when the scheme resumed after the war. Barnwell Manor, the home of the Duke and Duchess of Gloucester in Northamptonshire, and Coppins at Iver in Buckinghamshire, home of the Duchess of Kent and her children, were also opened.

Buckingham Palace was used constantly by the King and Queen to express their appreciation of the war effort, and to spur recovery in that drab and utility post-war world. The garden played a colourful part, with the revival of garden parties and many less formal occasions – such as on Friday 20 July 1951, in the Festival of Britain summer, when fifty Canadian schoolgirls came out of the Bow Room in a neat crocodile, across the terrace and onto the lawn:

> Standing there in summer tie-silk dresses in varying shades of
> colour but identical pattern, with fifty gay little hats all in exactly
> the same style perched on their heads, they looked very much like
> young ladies in the opening scene of some charming musical play.
> They made a very attractive picture on the palace lawn with the
> lake in the background and the tall, sheltering trees all round.

The Queen, in a lilac dress with a pleated skirt, and a big hat, worked her way around the circle, the girls bobbed, 'their silken dresses softly touching the grass', the Queen smiled endlessly, and the girls from 'the wastes of Yukon', from Yellowknife and Moosejaw and Medicine Hat each had a talk with her. The 'royal reporter' concludes: 'One of them as she came away showed me two daisies she had picked from the Palace lawn, "I shall send them back to Canada" she said.'[12]

Worn out with hard work and the worry of the war, King George VI died far too young, aged 56, in early 1952. His Queen was devastated – 'you could cut with a knife her desolation when the King died', her sister-in-law, Lady Bowes-Lyon, remembered.[13] Her discovery and restoration of the Castle of Mey in Caithness played a significant part in her recovery, and so did working in her gardens there and at Birkhall and Royal Lodge. The gardening world was soon at her feet, the Royal Horticultural Society gave her their highest accolade, the Victoria Medal of Honour, she regularly dined with the elite of horticulture and charmed them into laughter, she endlessly encouraged her gardening friends (especially those with rhododendron gardens) and relished the rivalries and triumphs of the show bench – whether it was at Sandringham Village Show or at Chelsea. Her love of flowers, of choice fresh vegetables and of gardens ran as a charmed strand through her long life.

Back at Buckingham Palace, unlike John Richard Stirling fifty years before him, Head Gardener Cole stayed on and saw his garden through the new Queen's Coronation summer of 1953, retiring at the end of the year.

On 1 January 1954 Fred Nutbeam started work; he was 40, a professional gardener who had left school at 13 and was trained in the traditional way, and had then been a working gardener until he joined the Royal Navy for his war service. In 1947 his navy connection had taken him to St Donat's Castle on the south Wales coast as head gardener at Atlantic College which undoubtedly recommended him to Prince Philip. Like Queen Victoria, the new Queen regnant had asked her husband to take charge of the royal estates.

Nutbeam, his very name seeming to make the sun shine, was to be head gardener for twenty-four years, and he is remembered by all of his successors (and gardeners are a notoriously critical breed) as 'the rejuvenator of the garden'. It was, first of all, a garden for a young and active family: a sandpit, swing and slide for Prince Charles and

'Her Majesty's Body Guards and Royal Companies Parade for the Golden Jubilee'. This unique event included the Gentlemen at Arms, the Yeomen of the Guard, the Military Knights of Windsor, the Royal Company of Archers and the Chelsea Pensioners, and gave the lawn a contemporary reprise of its role as a parade ground.

Fred Nutbeam, MVO, RVM, 1914–97.

Princess Anne were installed within easy reach of the North Terrace, and the sandpit – as the Prince of Wales mentioned from the stage during the second Golden Jubilee concert – is still there. Its wooden cover now hosts an abundance of lichens, including a rather rare *Physcia dubia*.[14] If the old formal Round Bed had not already disappeared, it did so now, though its name remains: this area now has masses of scented yellow azaleas and many fine hybrid rhododendrons, all grown into mature plants. On the opposite side of the gravel path which became The Queen's Walk (from her morning walks with her dogs), Nutbeam planned the long Herbaceous Border.

The 'great oaks from little acorns grow' tradition, started at the births of Prince Charles and Princess Anne, was continued with more acorn seedlings marking the births of Prince Andrew and Prince Edward; these were planted in the garden on 10 March 1969. The Prince of Wales planted a cut-leaved beech (*Fagus sylvatica* var. *heterophylla* 'Aspleniifolia') to mark his twenty-first birthday on 14 November that year. For The Queen and Prince Philip's Silver Wedding anniversary in 1972 Lord and Lady Astor of Hever gave them a border of silver plants: the silver theme – highly fashionable in horticultural terms – lingered for The Queen's 1977 Jubilee. The Royal Horticultural Society sent her a silver lime (*Tilia tomentosa*) which is outside the private apartments; and a special silver garden of scented lavenders, artemesias, helichrysums, verbascums and other grey leaves was also planted out. It was the work of Mrs Desmond Underwood, of Ramparts Nursery near Colchester, the pioneer of this fashion and author of *Grey and Silver Plants* (1971), who was known to the garden world as 'the Silver Queen'.

Fred Nutbeam MVO retired the year after the Silver Jubilee, to his native New Forest, where he died in 1997.[15] The previous year, for The Queen's seventieth birthday, a group of the brilliant orangey-red evergreen azalea 'Fred Nutbeam', raised by George Hyde of Ferndown in Dorset, had been planted in the garden. Nutbeam's garden was also the backdrop for Peter Coats's *The Gardens of Buckingham Palace*, published in 1978. David Mitchell was head gardener for six years from 1978, and another particularly fine plantsman, Thomas Deighton, followed from 1984 to 1990. Stuart Goldsworthy was in post for two years, to be followed by Mark Lane, who had joined the garden staff in 1979 when he was 19, in the year after Fred Nutbeam retired.

With The Queen's approval, the garden has assumed a different direction under Mark Lane's regime, but as a large garden – like an ocean liner – cannot be turned around quickly, the origins of these changes go back to the beginning of her reign. Despite the acquisition of that ultimate symbol of the modern pace of life, the helicopter landing-pad, which Prince Philip recalls using for the first time just before the Coronation, the garden throughout the twentieth century was still

Marjorie Lyon, botanical drawing of a branch of wild cherry, *Prunus avium*, from *The Queen's Hidden Garden*, 1984.

persistently private and little seen. Occasionally a botanically minded garden-party guest noted something of interest: a certain Mme Dussan saw one of the shyer members of the daisy family, 'Gallant Soldier' (*Galinsoga parviflora*), or so it was reported in 1917, the spiders were first recorded in 1929 by W.S. Bristowe, and in her 1953 book *Mirror of Flowers*, on the wild flowers she could find in London, D.M. Eastwood had made use of her visit to a garden party in 1950 to add seven species to her list. Other London botanists were becoming intrigued by the thought of the garden, and on 5 June 1956 four of them – J.C. Codrington, D.H. Kent, J.E. Lousley and D.C. McClintock – made a first recording visit. They found a '… haven walled off from the rest of the metropolis for over a century, well provided with water, bushes and other vegetation, free from public disturbance, and largely unexamined'[16] – a botanical time-capsule. Other visits followed, dozens of species were recorded, and a complete natural history survey took place from 1960 to 1963, the results being published by David McClintock in 1964.[17]

In the 1960s, lest it be forgotten, environmental consciences were being sharpened: another of Prince Philip's 'green' friends, Max Nicholson of the Nature Conservancy, organised the series of *Countryside in 1970* conferences that the Prince chaired, highlighting the pressures on species diversity and habitats in the modern countryside. Not to be outdone (and not actually excluded), London and other large cities spawned urban wildlife groups of ecologists, botanists and amateur naturalists (often the members of long-established entomological societies), who set out to prove their convictions that rich habitats were now to be found in post-industrial and post-war-damaged city sites.[18] In London, where the Clean Air Acts of 1956 and 1968 seriously improved air quality, they were certainly proved right, but as these same sites were clearly in many cases ripe for future development, the spotlight fell on urban parks and suburban gardens as vital preserves of species diversity. In this stream of thinking the garden of Buckingham Palace clearly emerged as a unique treasure-house.

This was popularly celebrated in Dr David Bellamy's *The Queen's Hidden Garden: Buckingham Palace's Treasury of Wild Plants*, published in 1984 and enchantingly illustrated by the botanical artist Marjorie Lyon.[19] The text is based upon the 1960–63 survey but, with characteristic aplomb, Bellamy whisks his readers off to distant realms – to pollen records to find that lime was dominant here during the Climatic Optimum of about 5000 BC; to the days of the St James's leper hospital surrounded with willowherbs, wild plum and blackthorn; and to cogitate on the opportunistic seeds, like the chamomile that found its way from Kensington Palace or Hampton Court. He proposes at least twenty-five species that might have arrived in gravel and soil from Kensington, Shirley Common or Norwood. He wittily highlights 'royal' connections – *Kickxia elatine*, the figwort known as 'Sharp-leaved Fluellen' from Shakespeare's *Henry V*, *Hieracium lepidulum* var. *haematophyllum*, an unusual hawkweed he named 'Queen's Own', and a silverweed, *Potentilla anserina*, with noticeably silver fern-like leaves, which he called 'Prince's Feathers'.[20]

A pile of logs and dry leaves provides a wonderful habitat for some of the garden's 287 species of beetle.

The Queen's Hidden Garden is a masterclass in botanical wizardry, for of course it conjures up an imaginative world that protects the fragile reality. The only observer to make regular visits to the garden for forty years was the distinguished botanist David McClintock (1913–2001), who was also a keen gardener and a grower of prize-winning heathers and who became, in 1995, a member of the select company of holders of the RHS's Victoria Medal of Honour.[21] Buckingham Palace garden was one of his many interests, and his consistent monitoring of the wild flowers there led to his colleagues from the London Natural History Society returning to the garden for a second survey in the mid-1990s at the invitation of Mark Lane.

Every garden should have a compost heap. Probably only one at a palace has to be turned using a JCB.

During his first five years as head gardener Mark Lane had been modifying the management regimes to balance the needs of wildlife and horticulture more equally: the main lawn had to be cut weekly through the growing season but other 'long grass' areas were cut only twice a year. Chemicals were kept to a minimum, being used only where and when absolutely necessary; most of the weeding was manual and fertilisers were used only on the ornamental lawns and shrubberies. A major innovation was the Recycling Centre at the Wellington Arch corner of the garden, a composter's delight where leaf-fall, lawn-cuttings and all green waste (formerly sent out of the garden) were sorted and converted into a rich mulch for the beds and borders. The Palace garden had become an experimental ground for the effectiveness of rich-habitat gardening.

The detailed results of the 1995–7 survey by more than two dozen expert recorders were published in two Supplements to *The London Naturalist*, in 1999 and 2001. Some of the gems from the close-printed texts are irresistible. Moths recorded included three species 'previously unknown from the British isles';[22] the beetle population had benefited greatly from the composting regime, with a total of 287 species (assessed as near to the maximum for such an urban site),[23] and the minuscule and elusive non-lichenised fungi – 630 species and at least two new to science – also thrive on the mulches, though the speedy removal by the gardeners of fallen branches and dead wood is a minus for the fungi.[24] The record of tardigrades – microscopic, multi-cellular invertebrates – was a first for Greater London, with 123 examples of eleven species, one new to Britain, another new to England.[25] The West Terrace with its balustrades and vases proved a good home for very small mosses, including the pollution-sensitive *Syntrichia intermedia*; and a rarity in southern England, *Bryum pseudotriquetrum*, was found amongst tangled tree roots at the lake edge. The numbers of mosses and liverworts, especially sensitive to pollution, dryness and active gardening, had doubled since the 1960s survey.[26] One visitor, the slug *Lehmannia valentiana* (so prettily named), an Iberian native first found in a greenhouse in Belfast Botanical Gardens in 1948, was 'firmly established', living outdoors in this warm London garden.[27]

Nesting species of birds included wren, dunnock, robin, blackbird and thrushes (although the number was disappointingly low for London sparrows); blackbird, wood pigeon and blue tit were the top three breeding species, closely followed by the wildfowl.[28] Roach, gudgeon and perch reside in the lake – an interestingly isolated habitat also affecting the frogs in the garden, perhaps coming through underground pipes. Of mammals the pipistrelle bats (possibly both known species) are the most important, but there are also grey squirrels, field voles, mice, rats and, though perhaps not now, the urban fox, at least as a one-time visitor.[29]

The Queen especially enjoys the wildfowl on her lake. Peter Scott, owner of the Wildfowl Trust at Slimbridge in Gloucestershire and a co-founder with Prince Philip of the World Wildlife Fund, sent her in late 1965 eight red-breasted geese, which bred successfully. They were joined by flamingoes from Kenya, of which everyone was particularly proud, at one time feeding them on shrimps and cockles from Billingsgate as their 'pink' diet until Slimbridge provided a dietary supplement. The lake is part of a 'London circuit' for free-flying birds, and various geese, ducks, swans, heron and cormorants come and go between Regent's Park, Kensington Gardens and the nearer St James's Park. Disaster struck in the autumn of 1995 when a fox took five of the six red-breasted geese, and worse still another raid killed all the flamingoes in January 1996. Every effort has been made since then to fox-proof the garden, but it was decided not to replace the flamingoes. Slimbridge sent two pairs each of red-breasted and Emperor geese and some ducks – mandarins and tufted included. Smew, goosander, shoveler, pochard and grebe and an occasional kingfisher also frequent the lake, along with the less desirable gulls.[30]

That leaves the gardeners' plants and the wild flowers. Of the latter the rarities include marsh pennywort, adder's-tongue, the round-leaved cranesbill *Geranium rotundifolium*, hare's foot clover and silver hair-grass. The 'Queen's Own Hawkweed' is a national rarity and has made a good colony, the common spotted orchid arrived in the Garden Yard and thrives in some iris pots, and the heracleum or giant hogweed, planted in Victorian times as an ornamental, is common in the garden but differs here from *H. mantegazzianum* and defies precise identification.[31] The 'long grass' groves farthest from the Palace have reverted to wild-flower meadows, rather as if the soil remembered the days when Queen Charlotte's house cows grazed here and the cream was skimmed and butter churned in the 'Queen's Dairy'.[32]

A pair of coots nesting on the lake.

Ducklings negotiating the steps of the new Queen Victoria Memorial en route from St James's Park to Buckingham Palace lake, June 1928.

Two greylag geese, browsing on the lawn outside the octagonal tea house. The rhododendron-lined Queen's Walk, leading to the Rose Garden, is just visible behind them.

LEFT AND ABOVE The success of the long-grass policy in the garden would be enough to convert the most ardent advocate of the lawn mower. Here bluebells jostle for space with the last of the daffodils, part of the policy of encouraging marginal plants around the lake's edge.

Opposite the gardeners' yard, when the old apple trees are in bloom, one might be in a wild-flower meadow rather than SW1. The long-grass areas of the garden include the Mound and around the lake, and they encircle the prim, Edwardian perfection of the Rose Garden and Waterloo Vase.

Looking through to the pieris,
rhododendrons and azaleas of the
Queen's Walk; and to the Arboretum
and Waterloo Vase.

The garden photographed by Christopher Simon Sykes for this book is, inasmuch as head gardeners are traditionally proprietorial, Mark Lane's garden. As head gardener since 1992 he has exhibited a knowledgeable flair for plantsmanship as well as a fine sense of history. He recalls that when he started work here in 1979 he was too shy even to look at the Palace; in the intervening years he has come to know the garden better than anyone else – everyone, that is, except The Queen, who first came to live here in 1937 when she was 10 years old. As her head gardener he has won her confidence and approval for the planting schemes he has put forward, particularly in bringing a more personal, human scale to the areas beyond the lawn, and every Monday morning when The Queen is in residence he sends her a posy of the interesting plants in flower.

For the last seven years the garden plantings have been recorded on a database, the first time that records have been kept. Particular attention is paid to the range of species that can be grown in this walled and sheltered city-centre garden where spring usually comes three weeks' earlier than in the outside world. Some of the rarer trees include a Chinese chestnut, *Castanea mollissima*; a round-leaved beech, *Fagus sylvatica* 'Rotundifolia'; the Chinese *Photinia beauverdiana* var. *notabilis* – with fine orange-red fruits and coloured autumn leaves; a golden Indian bean tree, *Catalpa bignonioides* 'Aurea'; and a particularly beautiful 'Pocket Handkerchief Tree', *Davidia involucrata*, given to The Queen and Prince Philip for the then young Prince Charles by the Metropolitan Public Gardens Association. A new cultivar, *Acer campestre* 'Queen Elizabeth', was a Golden Wedding present in 1997, along with a collection of golden roses, from Queen Beatrix of The Netherlands.

Pines make up only just over 2 per cent of the garden's species, but the several varieties of cedars and Scots pines are prominent: within the last ten years a Nootka cypress (*Chamaecyparis nootkatensis*), a bishop pine (*Pinus muricata*), Monterey and Bhutan pines, a swamp cypress and a *Taxus baccata* 'Dovastoniana' or Westfelton yew (the original planted at Westfelton in Shropshire in 1777, an especially beautiful wide-spreading tree with long horizontal branches and weeping branchlets), have all been planted.

Amongst the shrubs are the eccentric *Helwingia japonica*, with its green 'flower' and tiny black berries borne on the leaf like a cherry on a plate, and a precious, highly scented *Syringa x hyacinthiflora* 'Plena', Victor Lemoine's original cross of 1876. This plant is tucked away on the Mound and has clearly been there for a long time; it is fascinating to think that this may be the very 'Lilac Lemoineii flora plena' listed amongst shrubs supplied to the Palace garden in 1940 by Wood & Ingram's Nursery of Huntingdon, a firm in business from 1747 until 1950, with a huge clientele of far-flung and (clearly) distinguished customers. Nursery records so rarely survive that this order (there is also one for 10 Downing Street) seems too much of a coincidence to ignore. The 1940 shrub order has a strong emphasis on scented lilacs, philadelphus, honeysuckles, osmanthus and viburnums (some seventy plants for £12 10s. 0d.) and would seem to reflect the then Queen Elizabeth's love of scented flowering shrubs.[33]

The spirit of that order undoubtedly survives: the garden is rich in lilacs, roses, magnolias, camellias and hydrangeas, as well as azaleas and rhododendrons. The Rose Garden, formal beds of bush roses, was originally planted by the rosarian Harry Wheatcroft in the 1960s, and the varieties are continually updated. Old-fashioned shrub and species roses grow all around and behind the Admiralty summer house, with climbers on a Jekyll-style catenary rope. Especially successful varieties are *Rosa webbiana*, with its clear almond-pink flowers on slender arching branches; and the white, free-flowering 'ghost rose', *Rosa fedtschenkoana*. The rose named for The Queen's Silver Jubilee in 1977 is a rich red with a pink flush; it was raised by the Scottish breeder Alex Cocker.

Rhododendrons and azaleas were particular favourites of The Queen's father, King George VI. In retrospect the Wood & Ingram shrub order also reflects the difficult conditions of his times in the late 1930s, with the need to cut down on garden labour. The Round Bed, the complex circular layout of spring and summer bedding, which had been the most colourful feature of the garden since Aiton's time a century earlier, was cleared away – probably for the war effort – and never replaced. A plantation of yellow scented azaleas and the now magnificent hybrid rhododendrons reinstated the colour. A hybrid of one of the most famous of all rhododendrons, *Rh. Loderi* 'King George' (which was named for King George V) and the Edwardian 'Bulstrode Park' has recently been raised in the garden. It is named 'London Calling' (see page 171) and was presented to The Queen for her seventieth birthday by her gardeners.

ABOVE AND OPPOSITE *Helwingia japonica* is one of the most unusual shrubs in the garden; Victor Lemoine's original cross of 1876, *Syringa x hyacinthiflora* 'Plena', which grows on the Mound above the path leading from the gardeners' yard, is perhaps one of the oldest and rarest. On the left in the picture opposite, it is a reminder still of Queen Elizabeth The Queen Mother's preferences as a gardener.

FOLLOWING PAGES Both King George VI and Queen Elizabeth were very fond of rhododendrons and azaleas; the path leading to the Rose Garden has a particularly rich display. The vivid colours of the flowers stand out against the backdrop of the garden's perimeter belt of trees.

LEFT AND BELOW The extraordinary vivid green of a catalpa, growing on the edge of the Mound, and a weeping birch, planted in the 1960s.

OPPOSITE The exquisite golden colour of a fraxinus, growing by the lake, caught at the perfect moment in autumn, with aspen and dogwood to left and right.

FOLLOWING PAGES The lake in autumn. The colours of the trees around the lake are complemented by the deep green of *Gunnera maniculata*. Also visible are a yellow royal fern, *Osmunda regalis* (which was planted fifty years ago), and *Nyssa sylvatica*.

The belt behind the Herbaceous Border provides not only privacy but also
shelter for the many half-hardy or even tender plants in the border itself.

One of the spectacles of the garden now, especially for the July garden-party visitors, is the Herbaceous Border, which is 156 metres (512 feet) long and 5 metres (16 feet) deep. To the best of Mark Lane's knowledge, some of this area was used for wartime vegetables, and afterwards to cheer things up Fred Nutbeam planted bays of annuals. Of the next step Mark Lane has no doubts, recalling that it was his first job to dig and plant the border from scratch, the suggestion having come originally from The Queen's then Keeper of the Privy Purse, Sir Shane Blewitt. Understandably the border has been developed over the years; it has a bosky backdrop and a good south-west aspect, but – contrary to appearances – it is on entirely flat ground; the juxtaposition of plants creates both the ripple of colour and textures and the impression of a bank of flowers. Banana plants provide some of the richest foliage and they can be over-wintered here with merely a straw covering, an indication of the garden's Cornwall-like climate.

Since 1993 seven beds of plants native to North America have been developed in the area beyond the lake, where the summer visitors to the Palace pass as they are leaving. Part of this area once rejoiced in the name the 'mudhole' and lends itself to marginal and bog plants, including the umbrella plant, *Peltiphyllum* (sometimes *Darmera*) *peltatum*, with umbrels of pinkish flowers, as well as many varieties of trillium and ferns. There are also woodland and ericaceous beds – the former with birches, cornus, pistachio and buckeye; the latter with the wonderful American native azaleas, pieris, *Jamesia americana* of the hydrangea family with its star-shaped white flowers and the actaea or baneberry. The 'London Effect' allows *Clethra arborea*, with lily-of-the-valley-like flowers, *Arbutus canariensis*, the Chilean jasmine *Mandevilla laxa*, and even (though it is 'pushing the boundaries') the exquisite, magnolia-like *Michelia figo*.

'London Calling', the rhododendron cultivar raised in the garden at Buckingham Palace by the Palace gardeners, and presented to The Queen for her seventieth birthday.

Magnolia campbellii 'Alba' raises its star-like flowers into the sky above the gardeners' yard.

It perhaps should be added that many native shrubs – some that might be called weeds – are also cultivated in the garden, including guelder rose, the wayfaring tree, blackthorn and whitethorn, sea buckthorn, honeysuckles, goat willow, box and bearberry.

As if to come full circle in this history, the Palace garden has recently been granted provisional status as the holder of a national collection of mulberries. Twenty-nine varieties have been collected to date (though four of these are growing at Kensington Palace), many of them cultivars of *Morus alba*, the white mulberry – including the weeping 'Pendula', the curious long-lobed 'Laciniata' (also known as 'Skeletoniana') and one called 'Fruitless'. The collection spans the old world and the new and includes also two varieties of the rare *Morus rubra*, with rounded, downy leaves that turn vivid yellow in autumn. Twenty-nine varieties of this fascinating, legendary tree – the ghosts of the King's Mulberry Men, should they pass this way, would shake their heads in puzzlement.

5

They're changing guard at Buckingham Palace —
Christopher Robin went down with Alice,
They've great big parties inside the grounds.
'I wouldn't be King for a hundred pounds,' says Alice.

A.A. MILNE, 'BUCKINGHAM PALACE', *WHEN WE WERE VERY YOUNG*, 1924

5

PARTY GARDEN

George III and Queen Charlotte to Queen Elizabeth II

The Herbaceous Border, cause of many an intake of breath by guests at the summer garden parties. The border is 156 metres (512 feet) long and 5 metres (16 feet) deep. The section shown here includes two forms of helenium, hemerocallis, tradescantia, phlox, echinops, buddleia, nepeta (the humble catmint), and a banana plant.

THE VERY FIRST EVENT in the royal garden was a surprise party for George III, cleverly arranged in secret by Queen Charlotte as a triple celebration of his birthday, a thank-you and a house-warming. The royal birthday was celebrated on Saturday 4 June 1763 at St James's Palace, a masked ball bringing everyone to court and the company keeping the King occupied until the following Monday evening, when Queen Charlotte led him over to her new house – romantic accounts say he was blindfolded – up the Duke of Buckingham's great painted stairway and through to the rooms overlooking the garden front. The shutters were thrown back to reveal a triumphal arch and colonnade designed by Robert Adam (1728–92) and painted on canvas – this was called a transparency – so that it could be lit from behind by torches and candles. The drawn figures were often transformed into life-size cut-outs, operated as puppets; descriptions suggest that the decor was complicated by a false 'stage' over the lawn, with the puppets manipulated from underneath. The dark garden was transformed into something elaborately heroic – not unlike the contemporary but more permanent classical façade at Chatelherault outside Glasgow, which Robert's father, William Adam (1689–1748), had designed for the Duke of Hamilton about 1732, or William Kent's Temple of British Worthies of 1735 at Stowe. The combined ideals of military prowess and patriotism were the Queen's birthday presents to her 25-year-old husband, and they were duly endorsed with a musical entertainment and a grand supper supplied by her German confectioner Frederick Kuhffe.[1]

Queen Charlotte loved all animals and her small dogs came yapping and bouncing into her new house and garden; they were provided with their own stuffed green baize cushions, and Mrs Catherine Naish, Household joiner and chair-maker, made 'a Square Deal Tubb' for their baths. Mrs Naish also made the Queen a garden tent, there were new birdcages and 'two Mohogony Houses for a Turkey monkey'.[2] The Queen's most famous animal, the first zebra to be seen in England, was put on view to Londoners in a paddock on the former vegetable garden beside Buckingham Gate in the summer of 1762. The female zebra or 'a painted African ass', as *The London Magazine* called it, was presented to the Queen by Sir Thomas Adams, who had brought it home from the Cape of Good Hope in HMS *Terpsichore*. *The London Magazine* gave more details for the curious: 'the whole animal is striped with three colours, black, brown, and white; these are all very bright, and the hair is glossy; they turn cross wise of the body, but are not parted like the streaks of the tiger but surround the whole body' – in the accompanying painstaking illustration (see page 176) the zebra appears to be dressed in a jersey convict-suit.[3] George Stubbs relished the curiosity and made 'that likeness with an exact eye for conformation and markings, observing the animal with the same scientific detachment' as he brought to his other portraits of exotics, of rhinoceros, blackbuck and moose.[4] It has been suggested that Stubbs's background looks more like an English woodland than an African plain, hardly surprising if he is revealing the zebra's new home in the Buckinghams' rather overgrown garden.

Original Design of an Illumination & Transparency, part of which was executed by Command of the Queen in June 1762, in honour of His Majestys Birthday.
Dessein Original d'une Illumination et Transparence, dont une partie a été executée par Ordre de la Reine dans le Mois de Juin 1762, en honneur du Jour de la Naissance du Roi.

Design of a Bridge Illuminated in Honour of His Majestys Birth Day the 4th June 1763.
By Order of Her Majesty.

Robert Adam (1728–92), Design for an illumination for the King's Birthday, 1763. The illustration above shows an engraved perspective view of the general design for the illumination, and was included in *The Works in Architecture of the Late Robert and James Adam, Esqs.,* published in three volumes in 1822 (RCIN 1150278). The illustration below is one of Adam's originals of 1762, in pen and watercolour, showing a design for a bridge. RCIN 917643C

'The Queen's Female Zebra', as illustrated in *The London Magazine* for July 1762.

George Stubbs (1724–1806), *A zebra*, oil on canvas, 1763.

The London Magazine insisted that the zebra was 'one of the most inoffensive creatures in the world, feeds on grass and other vegetables and is gregarious. It brays loudly and harshly, like the common ass.' The zebra was joined by an elephant, a present to the King, which came with a keeper, Senetal, and his servant Newran; Senetal was attired in 'a rose lustrine Turkish robe and cap' and Newran in 'a chintz cotton mantle'. The elephant had 'a fringed blue cloth covering lined with red baize and a headpiece with a crown embroidered on either side'.[5]

The Queen's animals were among the sights of London for one or two summers but must then have been sent to the Tower – not for misdemeanours but because the royal menagerie had been kept there since Henry I's time; the first elephant in England arrived there in 1254, to join the first polar bear, which was regularly taken down to the River Thames to fish for its supper.[6] George III also kept wild animals at Windsor, most famously a cheetah, a present from the Governor of Madras, which refused to give a demonstration of catching its own supper. George Stubbs was called in to paint many of these celebrities, including the cheetah, and once – much to his disgust – the moose at Goodwood. This had died but was strung up to look alive for the painter. George IV had the first giraffe in the country at Windsor, where it survived for about two years. William IV sent all the remnants of the royal menageries to the newly formed Zoological Society gardens in Regent's Park.[7]

Gazelles, deer and Kashmiri goats were kept in Buckingham Palace garden in the 1840s and 1850s; on 17 June 1842 Queen Victoria wrote in her Journal of a type of gazelle 'bigger than the other, & equally tame, walking about in the garden & coming up to us to be stroked. They wear collars with little bells.' The Bey of Tunis presented more gazelles in 1846, and the Sultan of Morocco two more in 1850; some were undoubtedly kept at Buckingham Palace for the amusement of the royal children, and others were sent to Osborne and Windsor. Some of the Kashmiri goats were sketched in the garden by Friedrich Wilhelm Keyl, along with the gazelle, tame deer and water hens.[8]

The gazelle and the goats give a different image of the early Victorian garden, with at least the farther regions looking like a small park, with a browsing line to the trees; and the presence of the animals explains why at least one photograph shows the Round Bed and other borders of flowers strongly protected with decorative wire edging.

ABOVE Friedrich Wilhelm Keyl (1823–71), *Water hens in Buckingham Palace Gardens*, pencil and white chalk on cream paper, 1848. RL 23777

ABOVE RIGHT Friedrich Wilhelm Keyl, *Gazelle with chickens*, pencil and white chalk on cream paper, 1848. RL 23774

RIGHT Friedrich Wilhelm Keyl, *Indian goats*, pencil and white chalk on grey paper, 1848. Five goats with deer drawn in Buckingham Palace garden; the Queen's Kashmiri goats were part of a long tradition from Queen Charlotte to Queen Mary. The main flock was kept at Windsor and in Victoria's day their wool was woven into cashmere shawls as a cottage industry. In her Journal for 13 April 1844 the Queen noted that the flock had 'increased to the number of 49, including the kids, & look so pretty.' RL 23776

Queen Charlotte's dogs began a long canine cavalcade to lighten the mood of the garden and the cares of the monarchs. The young Queen Victoria's black spaniel Dash gave place to Prince Albert's greyhound Eos, the first 'female' in his life, whom the Queen wisely admired and respected. Eos came to England with Albert, she was sleek and black, except for her white muzzle, feet and tip to her tail and a white spot on the back of her head. She was his constant companion for more than ten years, and when she died in 1844 he must have felt he was losing a friend. There was also a wonderful Skye terrier, Corran, which belonged to Prince Alfred ('Affie'), Duke of Edinburgh, and was a great comfort to the widowed Queen in the late 1860s when she looked after the dog whilst Prince Alfred was at sea.[9] The garden then became terrier country (the gun-dog Labradors were always kept at Sandringham or Windsor), with King Edward VII's Jack and Caesar being followed by King George V's devoted Irish terriers. The Welsh corgis were introduced by King George VI and Queen Elizabeth; and the garden is corgi territory still.

A solitary corgi spots the photographer, and strikes a Landseer-like pose.

Edmund Cotterill (b.1765), for R. & S. Garrard, silver-gilt centrepiece of Queen Victoria's favourite dogs, 1842. This extraordinary piece was created from designs by Prince Albert, and shows on the left his greyhound, Eos, with Cairnach, a Skye terrier; on the right are Islay, a rough-haired terrier (also shown in Queen Victoria's sketch on page 72), and Waldman, a dachshund. RCIN 1570

In 1899 that great rosarian and Dean of Rochester, Samuel Reynolds Hole, opened his amusing gardening reminiscences, *Our Garden*, with a question that might prove useful here:

> I asked a schoolboy, in the sweet summertide 'What he thought a garden was *for*?' and he said, Strawberries. His younger sister suggested Croquet, and the elder Garden Parties. The (undergraduate) brother made a prompt declaration in favour of Lawn Tennis and Cigarettes, but he was rebuked by a solemn senior, who wore spectacles, and more black hair than is usual with males, and was told that 'a garden was designed for botanical research, and for the classification of plants'.[10]

The strawberries and garden parties are yet to come, the botanical and ecological researches have been included in Chapter 4, undoubtedly the garden has seen generations of strolling smokers, so that leaves the games – not overtly the subjects of official royal records but mentions have been found here and there. The young Queen Victoria and Prince Albert were outdoor addicts – skating in winter, including ice hockey for the men, and 'Ninepins' or skittles a summer favourite, played by all the family and the Queen with her ladies. The ninepins ground was clay hardened and rolled smooth, 25 feet long by 5 feet wide (7.6 by 1.5 metres), traditional skittles as played in alleys and back-yards all over Britain. There was also a lawn bowling-alley, and the 1869 Ordnance Survey shows a 'Gymnasium Pole' and a 'Swing Box' hidden amongst the trees – for private exertions in muscular development? When the Queen was absent so much in the 1870s her sons Affie and Arthur, Duke of Connaught, were allowed apartments in the Palace and it seems that cricket and football were often played on the lawn. Whether there was lawn tennis at this time is uncertain as the all-weather court installed in 1911 was one of the earliest in England. It has been constantly refurbished, most recently in 1998.

The sound of children's laughter does echo through the history of this garden from the days of Queen Charlotte's young family, though there were few around in the times of the old kings, George IV and William IV. Apart from what is known of Queen Victoria's and Prince Albert's love of games with their children, there is an 1854 photograph of nine healthily tousled boys, brought reluctantly to order from their game for their picture: but the tenth is the immaculately white-suited Prince of Wales, and his rather glum look emphasises that, even here in the garden, there were greater restrictions on royal children than on others. In later life the Prince was known for his zest and enthusiasm for organising impromptu games of cricket or ice hockey (these often on the lake

The Prince of Wales (later King Edward VII, seated dressed in white), Prince Alfred (in tartan socks) and friends in the garden at Buckingham Palace, 1854.

at Sandringham, which froze more regularly than the Palace lake) and in such instances he retained 'the heart of a schoolboy' even when he was King Edward VII.[11] His own children grew up with greater freedoms in the Sandringham gardens, and his sons inherited the King's love of the countryside and of country sports.

King George V's third son, Prince Henry of Gloucester, married Lady Alice Montagu-Douglas-Scott, the daughter of the Duke of Buccleuch, in 1935, and she has written a memoir of her childhood which recalls the atmosphere of London gardens in the early years of the twentieth century, and the freedoms of non-royal children. Lady Alice was one of eight brothers and sisters, and at their grand London home, Montagu House in Whitehall, with a garden running down to the Victoria Embankment, they had a lively time. Except when the 'grown-ups' had tea in the Chinese Pavilion (which is now preserved at Boughton House in Northamptonshire) on the lawn, the young 'seemed to have the whole place' to themselves:

> There were a few large plane trees, a catalpa tree, bushes and bordering flower-beds. The flowers were for the most part red geraniums and marguerites encircled by close-planted clumps of those little royal-blue plants one always sees in public gardens. All other London gardens that we visited looked exactly the same. At the far end there was a thick line of shrubs, a narrow path and then, bordering the Embankment, a seven-foot wall with a wide top.
>
> We children – thought to be safely out of mischief in the garden – would pile chairs against it and clamber up to watch the passing traffic on the street and the ships beyond, which were much more numerous in those days. We dangled wobbly wire spiders on long bits of elastic in the path of pedestrians below, skilfully whisking them up and ducking out of sight before our victims could spot us. There were always a number of pavement-artists sitting opposite, who could not have provided a more appreciative audience ...[12]

Princess Alice's nieces, the Princesses Elizabeth and Margaret Rose, were allowed to play freely in the Buckingham Palace garden because their mother, Queen Elizabeth, had had a fresh-air childhood of her own in Scotland and at St Paul's Waldenbury; she insisted upon the delights of picnics, hide-and-seek amongst the willow fronds and boating on the lake.

However, children have always been excluded from the garden parties. Queen Victoria began her outdoor parties ('breakfasts', as they were called) as court entertainments, but as occasions they were brilliantly perfected as part of the Golden and Diamond Jubilee celebrations in 1887 and 1897. After the great day of the Golden Jubilee, 21 June 1887, and the trip to the Abbey in a gilded landau through rapturously cheering crowds, the 68-year-old Queen was 'half dead with fatigue' and had to resort to her 'rolling chair' inside the Palace and only a partial view of the illuminations especially in her honour in St James's Park.[13] Next day was equally busy with her triumphal progress to Windsor, where she was allowed a few quieter days before returning to London on 29 June for the Jubilee garden party recorded in her Journal – after driving from Paddington station through still more enthusiastic crowds she reached the Palace:

> & before 5 I joined all my family (which is legion!) & the enormous number of foreign guests ... People were spread all over the garden, and there were a number of tents, and a large one for me, in front of which were placed the Indian escort. I walked right round the lawn in front of the Palace with Bertie, and I bowed right and left, talking to as many as I could, but I was dreadfully done up by it and could not speak to, or see, all those I wished.[14]

The Royal Collection includes a rich photographic record of these Jubilee parties in both formal and candid-camera shots. It was a perfect summer day on 29 June 1887, the lawn was crowded with elegant women – a sea of parasols and silk bustles – and uniformed or morning-coated escorts. The whole arrangement was splendid, there were banks of exotic flower arrangements around the large white marquee and the Queen's striped retiring tent, the latter guarded by magnificently dressed officers of Her Majesty's Indian regiments. An enormous fountain played on the lake,

This photograph from the 1880s shows the west front of the Palace still with Nash's original statues and finials in place along the parapet. These were later removed on safety grounds. Even more intriguingly, however, it also shows the determined march, two by two, across the lawn of the Palace, of pairs of sizeable and no doubt venerable trees, and it has been suggested that these could be survivors of Buckingham's 17th-century avenue of limes. The head of the fountain, seen in the oil painting of Queen Victoria's Diamond Jubilee garden party on page 186, can be seen just above the surface of the lake on the right of the photograph. RCIN 2101828

OVERLEAF Frederick Sargent (d.1899), *Queen Victoria's Golden Jubilee Garden Party, 29 June 1887*, oil on canvas, 1887–9. The Queen, with the Prince and Princess of Wales, may be seen in the centre of the painting. RCIN 407255

Queen Victoria's Golden Jubilee garden party, 29 June 1887:
OPPOSITE ABOVE The Queen's Guard on duty at the royal tent (detail).
OPPOSITE BELOW The Queen's retiring tent (detail).
ABOVE General view across the lake with the punts ready for the partygoers (detail).

which in its more peaceful stretches took on the semblance of a Venetian canal as the Queen's Watermen, in their distinctive uniforms, rowed or punted parties of guests around.

The Diamond Jubilee on 28 June 1897 was equally fine – 'Queen's weather' – and the arrangements were much the same, except the fashions had drifted towards what would be known as the Edwardian, with big leg o'mutton sleeves on long and lovely dresses that swept the lawns, bigger hats and the inevitable parasols. This time the Queen, who was nearing 80, was driven around the lawn in her garden landau so that she could see, and be seen by, as many people as possible.

The parties, those 'golden afternoons' that glow in the memories of turn-of-the-century England, were such a success that the Prince and Princess of Wales gave some of their own at Marlborough House, to which the Queen paid a briefer visit. Then, on his Coronation Day, King Edward VII invited the whole Coronation procession into Buckingham Palace garden for a review, at which the entire family, including his sailor-suited grandsons David and Bertie, were present. For King George V and Queen Mary, 'our garden party' was stretched to include an average of 12,000 guests in the early 1930s. These were the largest ever held.

Up until the Second World War the garden parties were the pinnacle of the London season, and as the season was the mecca for visitors from all over the Empire, they could be called world events. But unlike presentations, it was not possible to apply for tickets to them. They were court occasions embossed by the multi-culturism of the Empire, most of the people present would have met before, and the process by which each 10,000 or so arrived on the lawn was understandably intricate: something of this process will be revealed shortly.

Laurits Regner Tuxen
(1852–1927). *Queen
Victoria's Diamond Jubilee
Garden Party, 28 June 1897*,
oil on canvas, 1897–1900.
The Queen, accompanied
by the Princess of Wales, is
being driven around the
lawn to meet her guests.
The two children in the
foreground cannot be
identified with absolute
certainty, but as children
were normally not present
at garden parties, they are
almost bound to have been
members of the royal
family. The sailor-suited
little boy is therefore most
likely to be Prince Edward
of York, the future King
Edward VIII, while the
blonde-haired girl may be
Princess Victoria Eugenie
(Ena) of Battenberg (born
1887), the daughter of
Beatrice, Princess Henry of
Battenberg. RCIN 405286

Queen Victoria's Diamond Jubilee garden party, 1897, candid shots from the Duke of Connaught's album: the Royal Watermen were at the party to give pleasure trips on the lake. The fountain was especially for the garden party and not normally a feature of the garden.

Plan for the arrangement of tents for the 1900 garden party. This basic arrangement is still in use today.

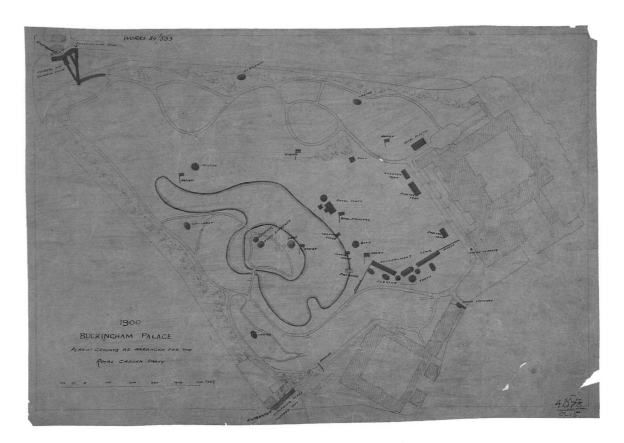

BELOW The first garden-party tents of the summer appear on the lawn, under the Indian chestnuts. The pair of tents shown here are used by the band, who alternate during the garden party from one to the other.

From King Edward VII's Coronation Album. The King and Queen Alexandra taking the salute of the Coronation Procession on their lawn in 1902 (detail). The sailor-suited Princes Edward and Albert (David and Bertie) come to the front for a better view.

FOLLOWING PAGES The border from early spring to high summer. Looking across to The Queen's private entrance to the garden. The border in early spring reveals the framework of plants that as the season progresses will develop into a spectacle of colour and mass (overleaf). By summer the illusion of rising height from front to back of the border is so convincing that most visitors insist it must be planted on a bank. This photograph was taken just before the gardeners began staking the plants.

ABOVE AND OPPOSITE The sweet peas (grown at Windsor) climb up metal or netting columns, to provide fragrance and height at the back of the border. The border itself is designed to display the maximum selection of herbaceous plants, with no repetition.

The border as seen from the north terrace outside
The Queen's private apartments, and (overleaf),
all 156 metres (512 feet) of it, at the pinnacle of
perfection in time for the garden parties in July.
The path leads to the Rose Garden.

Less publicised were the quieter garden occasions, enjoyed by very different groups of people. In May 1855 Queen Victoria presented medals to veterans of the Crimean War on Horse Guards Parade; the soldiers, sailors and marines were invited to the garden, given dinner in the Riding School, and then joined by the Queen for a band concert on the lawn. King George V and Queen Mary continued to invite war veterans, nurses and the 'landworkers' to such special garden occasions, and in May 1945 King George VI and Queen Elizabeth held parties for repatriated prisoners of war from all over the world. These smaller parties had a nostalgically traditional tea of brown and white bread and butter, Dundee and Madeira cake, Swiss roll and wine biscuits, with tea, coffee or home-made lemonade, all topped out with gateaux and vanilla ice cream – these last would have been surprise luxuries in 1945. Since then the 'special' garden party has continued, not automatically but at The Queen's pleasure: it has been timed to utilise the tents from the big garden parties but retains a distinct and rather informal atmosphere. In recent years such parties have been given for the Crown Estates Commissioners and their tenants and employees, the British Red Cross Society, the Not-Forgotten Association, and the Yeomen Warders of the Tower of London and their families.

Garden parties are feats of organisation. During the inter-war years the lists of invitees were drawn up through the previous winter and submitted to the King and Queen for approval; this entailed letters and memoranda flying backwards and forwards between the Palace and all the departments and ministries of state, the Houses of Parliament, the embassies and the armed and civilian services in order to match names to their allocations of the most distinguished and deserving of their personnel, a true collation of the great and the good. The rules were strict and deftly applied: an eagle eye was kept on legal notices in the newspapers for any breach of conduct that might precipitate the cancellation of an invitation; the forbidden applications were politely discouraged, though proposals were always considered. It was a business conducted between friends or at least acquaintances (the Royal Military College at Sandhurst was the most likely Alma Mater for all concerned); Susan Tweedsmuir, wife of the novelist John Buchan, who was Governor-General of Canada, might successfully intervene for her son William Buchan (wives and/or daughters were invited but sons usually had to fend for themselves), but Margot, Countess of Oxford and Asquith, widow of the Prime Minister, was firmly told on proposing her couturier in 1938 that he was not included 'amongst those to whom Their Majesties would wish to extend hospitality'.[15] That same couturier subsequently dressed many royal ladies – and attended many garden parties.

The arrival of the stiff white card invitations, beautifully written in voluminous copperplate, *The Lord Chamberlain is commanded by Their Majesties to invite ... To an Afternoon Party in the Garden of Buckingham Palace ...* was always a cause of great excitement. The research was so accurate that the rate of acceptances (a record was carefully kept and regularly shown to the King) was usually over

E. Moreton (fl.1855), *Crimean war veterans being entertained in the garden, 18 May 1855*, watercolour. RCIN 16784

OPPOSITE Jubilee of the Queen's District Nurses' Association – the parade of 2,000 nurses in the garden, 16 June 1937.

70 per cent of some 15,000 or 16,000 invitations issued. Conversely, the inability to accept, unless it was by being abroad, was likely to blot one's social escutcheon; it was quite usual to put a notice in the Court Circular explaining an unavoidable absence caused by a broken leg or similar accident.

In those days of Empire the Indian contingent was prominent, both because of the government's treaty obligations to various princes and for their magnificently costumed appearances. The Indian 'notabilities' stood a good chance of being presented, though formal presentations at garden parties were few – and the lists of those attending were annotated with vital information. One of the most charming, for King George V in 1931, was for Risaldar-Major Gulam Muntaza of the Hyderabad Lancers, who had 'once carried His Majesty on his back across a river in Hyderabad'[16] and retained a photograph of the occasion.

The white invitation card (which could be retained on the mantelpiece) was accompanied by the vital admittance card, to be surrendered at the Palace gates, and even in the 1920s these were carefully checked against the lists of invitations. Three passes were issued for photographers of *The Times* to go up onto the roof of the Palace in 1925; the number steadily increased in later years. The Master of the Household dealt with the practicalities of the presence of 11,000, on the whole elderly rather than young, people crowded on the lawn on a hot afternoon; the attendance of the St John Ambulance Brigade and the Red Cross was an important consideration. Occasionally old-world courtesy springs from the files – such as a note in the strong hand of Constance, Lady Battersea, a clever and charitable woman and a great garden-maker, who offered '1,000 thanks' to

Sir Derek Keppel for her enjoyment of the garden, particularly because she had been provided with a 'bath chair'.[17]

The vast tea tents provided by Solomons of Aldershot (and later by Benjamin Edgington) were arranged around the lawn so that they could be supplied discreetly from 'backstage' via the perimeter pathways. Every so often someone thought they had come up with a better arrangement, but the original plan was always readopted. For decades the catering was masterminded by Mr Bertie Joseph of J. Lyons & Company, owners of the swish Trocadero Restaurant in Piccadilly Circus as well as of the popular Lyons Corner Houses, and caterers to Wimbledon Lawn Tennis Championships and other glamorous occasions. Maestro Joseph brought mass-catering to a fine art, exactly 420 feet (about 122 metres) of buffet would serve 11,000 guests, but this could be extended by another 100 feet (30 metres) to serve 13,500, which was tried in 1939. However, this was deemed too crowded and it was later decided that two main parties were the solution.

Lyons's tea was unchangingly sumptuous, a feast of cucumber and salmon sandwiches and filled bridge rolls, plain brown and white bread and butter, scones, strawberry tarts, macaroons, florentines, Dundee and Madeira cakes, Swiss roll, gateaux, Indian and China tea, hot and iced coffee and home-made lemonade. Everything originated at the Cadby Hall cream-cake factory in the Hammersmith Road. Mr Joseph's proudest moment was probably when he escorted Queen Mary, and subsequently Queen Elizabeth, on a tour of inspection of the buffet prior to the guests' arrival. All was – and remains – immaculately 'silver service' with the delicate sandwiches and cakes protected beneath their glistening covers.

Music was an important part of the garden-party atmosphere, provided by a band from one of the regiments of which the Sovereign was colonel-in-chief, meaning usually a Guards band and a second band from a provincial or territorial regiment. The sounds of Vaughan Williams's 'English Folk Song Suite', Holst's 'Jupiter', Eric Coates's 'Summer Days', Strauss waltzes, Verdi, Chopin, Donizetti and of course Gilbert and Sullivan's musical scores, drift across the lawn and through the willow branches beside the lake. On fine days, and they usually seem to have been blessedly fine, it was all perfect, and meant to be so: the apotheosis of the garden party as performed on lesser lawns from Stow-on-the-Wold to Simla, an essential part of the traditions of summer.

A guest at the children's party held in the garden to celebrate the fiftieth anniversary of The Queen's Coronation, 2 June 2003.

Changes in society were reflected in the lists of invitees when the garden parties were resumed after the Second World War. Members of the medical professions were included, plus some heads of schools and colleges, and in the year of the Wembley Olympics (1948) some of the visiting competitors. Invitations also went out to the clergy and tenants on the royal estates. Ties with the Commonwealth remained very strong; in 1969 the list of presentations from India was headed by Mr and Mrs Dilip Kumar, the film stars, and Tripti Das, the classical singer.

All through the present Queen's reign the guest lists have become purposefully ever more democratic. The Lord Chamberlain's invitation now falls through the letterboxes of guests in all walks of life, causing both consternation and delight. Guests are invariably invited with others they know and given sufficient notice to organise what for many will be the day of their year, if not of a lifetime. The invitation and admission cards are now accompanied by other essential information, such as which of the entrances to use (the Grand Entrance, the Garden Entrance on the north side of the Palace, and the Hyde Park Corner and Grosvenor Gates are opened), some notes on the garden and the afternoon's timetable. Invitations are for 3 o'clock and tea is served from

One of the more unusual sights of London in 2003 – a merry-go-round on the lawn of the Palace for the children's party.

3.30; after the Yeomen of the Guard have 'held ground' and come on parade for their afternoon duties, and at 4 o'clock sharp, The Queen and Prince Philip and other members of the Royal Family come out onto the terrace and presentations are made. Then The Queen leads the way through 'lanes' of guests (circles have been tried), meeting as many people as possible. Guests with tickets for the Royal Tea Tent adjourn there at 4.45 and The Queen joins them about half an hour later; the National Anthem closes the party at 6 o'clock.

These annual parties of the third week in July remain the high points of the garden's year. There used to be a lull whilst the Royal Family were on holiday in Scotland, but now the garden is seen by thousands more visitors to the Palace during the Summer Opening. For The Queen's Golden Jubilee in 2002, the two celebrity concerts held in June were each attended by 10,000 guests seated on the lawn. These magnificent occasions were seen around the world on television but of course did not happen overnight. They required months of preparation, followed by weeks of clearing up. Much less trying for the lawn was the special party held on the fiftieth anniversary of The Queen's Coronation on 2 June 2003. On that sunny afternoon 500 children – invited through Barnardo's; the Soldiers', Sailors' and Air Force Association's Forces Help; and the London Taxi Drivers' Fund for Underprivileged Children – arrived at the Palace. They had the time of their lives on the lawn, with roundabouts and swings, candyfloss and ice cream, clowns and balloons, and the band of the Coldstream Guards played lively party music, including the theme from *Star Wars*.

During the late summer of 2003 keen-eyed visitors may have noticed some necessary excavation trenches crossing the garden: a watching brief was kept on these works by archaeologists, who hoped to identify the line of Civil War earthwork defences known to have been built across the garden whilst Lord Goring was in exile, and evidence of the wall which Lord Arlington built around the Great Garden in the late 1670s or early 1680s. The evidence was found – tangible confirmation winging across the centuries to verify events more than 350 years ago.

The garden can be imagined as the oldest part of Buckingham Palace, pre-dating even the Duke of Buckingham and his house. As groves with nightingales and green and quiet glades do not

'The Party at the Palace', one of the two concerts held in the garden in 2002 as part of the celebrations of The Queen's Golden Jubilee. Here Brian May kicks off the proceedings with a rendition of 'God Save The Queen' from the roof of the Palace, a virtuoso performance that rolled back almost four hundred years to when the figures of Apollo, Liberty, Mercury, Equity, Truth and Secrecy danced around the Duke of Buckingham's roof; The Queen appears on stage at the end of the concert with The Prince of Wales and some of the performers; and the crowd celebrates in The Mall.

develop overnight, its atmosphere was evolving well before it became a royal residence almost two-and-a-half centuries ago. It was, as this history has emphasised, the very position of 'this favourite spot of Ground' that ensured its singular fate; even in the eighteenth century location was all, and the garden at the end of The Mall was propelled into history.

The Duke of Buckingham loved his garden (gardens being a weakness of worldly men, particularly politicians) and later owners seem to have followed suit. Even those who have become disillusioned with Buckingham Palace itself (William IV who wanted to give it away, Queen Victoria who neglected it, King George V who despairingly suggested selling it) seem to have had quite different feelings about the garden. It is perfectly true to say that gardens thrive on love, especially as gardeners as a breed enjoy their work, and impart this into long centuries of labour. As a walled oasis, this garden has grown in real and intangible ways into a green space of innocent enchantment. It is unique. It is quite unlike any other royal garden, and it is certainly not in step with the conventional 'great gardens' of which Britain is so proud. And yet it is probably worked harder, fulfils more roles and gives pleasure to more people than any of them.

But for all the garden's fascinating evolution inside its walls, which has been the main story of this book, it also holds a mirror-image from the outside world. As a city-centre garden it is unique: it harbours within its green shades a memory of a forgotten London, the London of when the garden was young, and when the City of Westminster was approached through lanes and meadows. More prosaically, it holds Buckingham Palace as the oyster-shell holds the pearl: together and inseparably they are the heart of ceremonial London. Palaces are many, but a palace in a garden in the heart of a great city is one of the rarest of treasures.

Under the lime trees. The essential ingredients of any English garden – grass, sunshine and dappled shade. The same qualities have remained unchanged in the garden since Queen Victoria described them in a letter to her uncle Leopold of 1841.

NOTES AND FURTHER READING

The primary and published sources given in these notes are as used by the author. Where quotations and other details are from sources in the Royal Archives and have been published, the published sources are given.

Historical documentation concerning Buckingham Palace is chiefly divided between the Royal Archives (particularly the Privy Purse records) at Windsor Castle and The National Archives (formerly the Public Record Office) at Kew. The latter is the repository of the records of government departments. The History of the King's Works, published in six volumes under the general editorship of Sir Howard Colvin (London, 1963–73) is the official history of one of these departments – the Office of Works; it contains much useful information on the building history of Buckingham Palace and adjacent areas.

Introduction

1 A.A. Milne's 'Buckingham Palace', *When We were Very Young*, 1924. Virginia Woolf, *Mrs Dalloway*, 1996, p. 7

2 The Queen's Palace and Richmond, indenture dated 20 April 1763, p. 22, RCIN 1150274

3 Peter Willis, *Charles Bridgeman and the English Landscape Garden*, 2002, p. 104, quoting Horace Walpole, *Walpoliana*, 1799

4 Roy Strong, *Royal Gardens*, 1993, p. 55, quoting George Vertue (1684–1756), whose notebooks on art history were published by the Walpole Society, 6 vols., 1929–52.

5 Francis Bacon (1561–1626), Essay No. XLVI, 'On Gardens', 1597, from *Francis Bacon Selections*, eds. P.E. and E.F. Matheson, 1952, p. 95

6 Geoffrey Jellicoe, *Studies in Landscape Design*, vol. 3, 1966, p. 1

7 RA MRH/HH 1/140, 1881–2, correspondence regarding Brodrick Thomas's proposals, see Chapter 2, n. 27

8 David McClintock, O.W. Richards and M. Knight, 'Natural History of the Garden of Buckingham Palace', *Proceedings and Transactions of the South London (Entomological & Natural History) Society*, 1964. The recent surveys are detailed in *The Natural History of Buckingham Palace Garden, London*, parts 1 and 2, ed. Colin W. Plant, and published as supplements to *The London Naturalist*, nos. 78, 1999, and 80, 2001.

Chapter 1: An Accident of Design

Opening quotation: The Queen's Palace and Richmond, indenture dated 20 April 1763, p. 22. RCIN 1150274

1 The house was acquired in 1762, with the Treasury sanctioning building work there in July 1762. (See Howard Colvin, *The King's Works*, V, p. 134, n. 4.)

2 Jasper Ridley, *Elizabeth I*, 1987, pp. 20–21

3 There are many versions of this well-worn history; I have agreed with Edna Healey, *The Queen's House: a Social History of Buckingham Palace*, 1997, pp. 2–3; but see also J. Edgar Sheppeard, *Memorials of St James's Palace*, 1894, vol. I, p. 20 *et seq*, and Colvin, *The King's Works*, vol. IV, part II, pp. 241–3.

4 Guy Williams, *The Royal Parks of London*, 1985, p. 64; and Charles T. Gatty, *Mary Davies and the Manor of Ebury*, vol. 1, 1921, p. 15

5 Healey, *The Queen's House*, p. 4

6 Healey, *The Queen's House*, pp. 3–4

7 Gatty, *Mary Davies*, p. 108

8 Healey, *The Queen's House*, p. 10, quoting *Pepys's Diary*, ed. H. Wheatley, 8 vols., 1924, entry for July 1660

9 Gatty, *Mary Davies*, p. 108

10 Roy Strong, *The Renaissance Garden in England*, 1979, p. 194

11 Strong, *The Renaissance Garden*, p. 191

12 Laurence Pattacini, 'André Mollet, Royal Gardener in St James's Park, London', *Garden History*, vol. 26, no. 1, 1998, pp. 3–18

13 Strong, *The Renaissance Garden*, p. 200

14 Healey, *The Queen's House*, p. 4

15 Healey, *The Queen's House*, p. 9

16 Healey, *The Queen's House*, p. 10, quoting *Pepys's Diary*, ed. Wheatley, entry for May 1668

17 Jacob Larwood, *The Story of the London Parks*, 1872, p. 377

18 Philip Francis, ed., *John Evelyn's Diary*, 1963, pp. 170–71, entry for 1 March 1671

19 Edmund Waller, 'On St James's Park as Lately Improved by His Majesty', *The Works of the English Poets*, ed. A. Chalmers, 1810, vol. 3; quoted in *The Oxford Book of Garden Verse*, ed. John Dixon Hunt, 1993.

20 Sheppeard, *Memorials of St James's Palace*, p. 22, quoting Pepys's entry for 9 February 1665

21 Waller, 'On St James's Park', as n. 19 above

22 John Wilmot, Earl of Rochester, 'A Ramble in St James's Park', *The Complete Poems*, ed. D.M. Vieth, 1974, quoted in *The Oxford Book of Garden Verse*, pp. 66–7.

23 Peter Coats, *The Gardens of Buckingham Palace*, 1978, p. 24

24 Frances Harris, 'The Manuscript of John Evelyn's "Elysium Britannicum"', *Garden History*, vol. 25, no. 2, 1997, pp. 131–7

25 John Dryden (1631–1700), 'Arlington House', quoted in Coats, *The Gardens of Buckingham Palace*, pp. 27–8

26 'There are six of the greatest earthen pots that are anywhere else, being at least ten feet [3 metres] over within the edge', quoted in Coats, *The Gardens of Buckingham Palace*, p. 29.

27 Dryden, 'Arlington House', quoted in Coats, *The Gardens of Buckingham Palace*, p. 29

28 The Queen's Palace and Richmond, RCIN 1150274: trustees of Charles, Duke of Grafton, confirmation of legacy of Arlington House to John, Marquess of Normanby, 27 May 1698.

29 Coats, *The Gardens of Buckingham Palace*, p. 29

30 Celia Fiennes, 'London and the Later Journeys (*c*.1701–3), Westminster and the Royal Funerals and Coronations', in which she notes at St James's 'one Nobleman's house in this, Parke House', adding a marginal note, 'Arlington, now the Duke of Buckinghams being newly built'. *The Journeys of Celia Fiennes*, introd. John Hillaby, 1983, pp. 333–4 and p. 404, n. 2.

31 David Green, *Gardener to Queen Anne: Henry Wise (1653–1738) and the Formal Garden*, 1956, p. 92

32 David Green, 'Blenheim: the Palace and Gardens under Vanbrugh, Hawksmoor and Wise', *Blenheim: Landscape for a Palace*, eds. James Bond and Kate Tiller, 2nd edn., 1997, p. 73. Wise took the motto from Matthew 10:16.

33 David Green, entry for Henry Wise in *The Oxford Companion to Gardens*, eds. P. Goode and M. Lancaster, 1986, p. 610

34 The descriptions of Buckingham's garden are from John Sheffield (1648–1721), *The Works of John Sheffield, Earl of Mulgrave, Marquis of Normanby and Duke of Buckingham*, 1723, 2nd edn., corrected 1729, printed and sold by Aaron Ward etc., 'A Letter to the D—— of Sh——', p. 253 *et seq*.

35 Coats, *The Gardens of Buckingham Palace*, p. 38

36 David Jacques, *Georgian Gardens: the Reign of Nature*, 1983, p. 75

37 Nikolaus Pevsner, *The Englishness of English Art*, 1978, p. 53

38 Dorothy Stroud, *Capability Brown*, 1984, pp. 122–3

39 Linda Colley, *Britons: Forging the Nation 1707–1837*, 1992, p. 197, quoting John Brooke, *George III*, 1972, p. 108

40 David Coombs, 'The Garden at Carlton House of Frederick Prince of Wales and Augusta Princess Dowager of Wales', *Garden History*, vol. 25, no. 2, 1997, p. 165

41 Horace Walpole to Lady Ossory, quoted in Stroud, *Capability Brown*, p. 201

42 Stroud, *Capability Brown*, pp. 164–5, quoting Chambers's 'Dissertation on Oriental Gardening', 1772

43 John Summerson, *The Life and Works of John Nash, Architect*, 1980, pp. 161–2

44 Stephen Daniels, *Humphry Repton: Landscape Gardening and the Geography of Georgian England*, 1999, p. 121

45 Daniels, *Humphry Repton*, p. 202

46 Daniels, *Humphry Repton*, p. 205

47 John Martin Robinson, *Buckingham Palace: the Official Illustrated History*, 2000, p. 65

48 Robinson, *Buckingham Palace*, pp. 92–3

49 Marie Busco, *Sir Richard Westmacott Sculptor*, 1994, pp. 55–7

50 'The Waterloo Vase', by W.H., in *Naval and Military Magazine*, vol. II, 1827, pp. 368–73

51 Robinson, *Buckingham Palace*, p. 55

52 Robinson, *Buckingham Palace*, p. 62

53 *The Gardeners' Gazette*, ed. George Glenny, no. 504, 11 August 1838

54 J. Dennis, *The Landscape Gardener; comprising the History and Principles of Tasteful Horticulture*, 1835, pp. 103–5

55 Frank Pagnamenta, 'The Aitons: Gardeners to Their Majesties, and Others', published in three editions of *Richmond History, Journal of the Richmond Local History Society*, nos. 18, 1997; 19, 1998; 20, 1999; part 3, no. 20, 1999, p. 37.

56 Robinson, *Buckingham Palace*, p. 62

57 Robinson, *Buckingham Palace*, p. 68

58 Elizabeth Longford, *Victoria RI*, 1971, p. 83, quoting Thomas Carlyle

Chapter 2: Precious Privacy

Opening quotation: King George V's Diary, 22 February 1912; quoted in Kenneth Rose, *King George V*, 1983, p. 137

1 Peter Willis, *Charles Bridgeman and the English Landscape*, 2002, p. 104, quoting Horace Walpole, *Walpoliana*, 1799

2 Horace Walpole, *Memoirs of the Reign of King George III*, ed. Derek Jarrett, 2003, p. 103

3 Dorothy Stroud, *Capability Brown*, 1984, pp. 126–7

4 *Frogmore House and the Royal Mausoleum*, Royal Collection, 2000, pp. 34–5

5 John Martin Robinson, *Buckingham Palace: the Official Illustrated History*, 2000, p. 84

6 Claire Tomalin, *Mrs Jordan's Profession: the Story of a Great Actress and a Future King*, 1995, p. 309

7 Wilfrid Blunt and William T. Stearn, *The Art of Botanical Illustration*, 1994, p. 252

8 Queen Victoria to King Leopold of the Belgians, 11 July 1837, from Christopher Hibbert, *Queen Victoria in her Letters and Journals*, 2000, p. 25

9 *The Gardeners' Gazette*, ed. George Glenny, no. 504, 11 August 1838

10 Geoffrey Taylor, *The Victorian Flower Garden*, 1952, p. 111

11 David Cecil, *Melbourne (The Young Melbourne and Lord M in one volume)*, 1955, pp. 281, 323

12 Prince Albert, letter of 13 April 1859 to the Princess Imperial of Russia, quoted in Theodore Martin, *The Life of HRH The Prince Consort*, 3rd edn., 1875, vol. 1, pp. 323–4.

13 RA VIC/Y 90/20, Queen Victoria to King Leopold of the Belgians, 31 May 1841

14 Queen Victoria's Journal, 20 June 1887, quoted in Hibbert, *Queen Victoria in her Letters and Journals*, p. 304

15 Elizabeth Longford, *Victoria RI*, 1971, p. 311

16 RA VIC/Y 98/5, Queen Victoria to King Leopold of the Belgians, 22 February 1853

17 Prince Albert to Duchess Caroline of Saxe-Gotha-Altenburg, 12 February 1841, quoted in Edna Healey, *The Queen's House: a Social History of Buckingham Palace*, 1997, p. 136

18 RA VIC/C 26/38, Office of Woods & Forests to Prince Albert, 15 July 1842

19 Edward Blore had been working on 460 sheets of designs including every kind of garden building, ornamental and functional, for Worsley Hall near Manchester. See Jane Brown, *The Art and Architecture of English Gardens: designs from the Collection of the Royal Institute of British Architects, 1609 to the Present Day*, 1989, pp. 96–7. Robinson in *Buckingham Palace*, p. 106, opts for Blore.

20 Howard Colvin, *The King's Works*, VI, p. 277

21 From the introduction by Mrs Jameson to *The Decorations of the Garden-Pavilion in the Grounds of Buckingham Palace under the Superintendence of L. Gruner*, published by Murray, Longman, Colnaghi, F.G. Moon and L. Gruner, Regent Street, London, 1845. RCIN 708005

22 Philip Magnus, *King Edward the Seventh*, 1967, pp. 93–4

23 Quoted in Magnus, *King Edward the Seventh*, p. 135

24 Letter of 24 August 1846 to *The Times* signed 'Sphinx'; see Healey, *The Queen's House*, p. 159

25 Colvin, *The King's Works*, VI, p. 287

26 Healey, *The Queen's House*, p. 165, quoting Frieda Arnold, *My Mistress the Queen*, trans. Sheila de Bellaigue, 1994, p. 51

27 RA MRH/HH 1/140, Correspondence etc., 1881–2 on replanting belts of trees along Grosvenor Place and Constitution Hill, between Queen Victoria and Sir John Cowell; and Cowell with Thomas Jones of the Royal Gardens, Windsor, and William Brodrick Thomas of 52 Wimpole Street, London.

28 *Journal of Horticulture*, vol. 34, 1897, pp. 543–66, article on royal gardens by S. Arnott

29 Robinson, *Buckingham Palace*, p. 125

30 Magnus, *King Edward the Seventh*, quoting Dowager Empress Marie Feodorovna of Russia to Tsar Nicholas II, 13 March 1907, p. 476

31 *Journal of Horticulture*, 13 March 1902

32 RA PP/EVII/A 9458 6/7 May 1902, Correspondence between the Earl of Denbigh and Sir Francis Knollys (the King's Private Secretary)

33 Magnus, *King Edward the Seventh*, p. 558

34 James Pope-Hennessy, *Queen Mary (1867–1953)*, 1959, p. 432

35 Healey, *The Queen's House*, p. 213

36 Pope-Hennessy, *Queen Mary*, p. 30

37 Pope-Hennessy, *Queen Mary*, p. 112

38 Pope-Hennessy, *Queen Mary*, p. 266

39 Pope-Hennessy, *Queen Mary*, p. 461

40 Kenneth Rose, *King George V*, 1983, p. 137

41 Queen Mary to Grand Duchess Augusta of Mecklenburg-Strelitz, 10 May 1915, in Pope-Hennessy, *Queen Mary*, p. 497

42 King George V's Diary: 6 May 1935, in Pope-Hennessy, *Queen Mary*, p. 555

43 Queen Mary's Diary: 1 October 1936, in Pope-Hennessy, *Queen Mary*, p. 571

44 Philip Ziegler, *King Edward VIII: the Official Biography*, 1990, p. 243

45 Ziegler, *King Edward VIII*, p. 253, quoting Sir John Reith, *Diaries*, p. 187

46 Ziegler, *King Edward VIII*, p. 250

47 Lady Bowes-Lyon in *The Queen Mother Remembered: the Intimate Recollections of her Friends 1900–2002*, ed. James Hogg and Michael Mortimer, 2002, pp. 72–5

48 M.D. Peacock, *The Story of Buckingham Palace*, 1951, quoted by S.M. Kett and R.S. Kirk in *The Natural History of Buckingham Palace Garden*, no. 78, 1999, p. 49

49 Healey, *The Queen's House*, p. 303, quoting letter from Queen Elizabeth to Queen Mary, 13 September 1940

50 Metropolitan Police, General Instructions for the Royal Palaces, 26 February 1932, and additional information kindly supplied to the author by PC Alex Garty, Royalty Protection, Buckingham Palace.

Chapter 3: The House at the Top of The Mall

Opening quotation: Noël Coward on Princess Margaret and Anthony Armstrong-Jones's wedding, 6 May 1960. *Noël Coward's Diaries*, eds. G. Payne and Sheridan Morley, 1982, entry for Sunday 8 May 1960, 'Hurrah for England Week', p. 438; quoted in Robert Lacey, *Royal*, 2002, p. 213

1 David Green, *Gardener to Queen Anne: Henry Wise (1653–1738) and the Formal Garden*, 1956, p. 92

2 Jacob Larwood, *The Story of the London Parks*, 1872, pp. 377–8

3 The quotations in this paragraph are from Guy Williams, *The Royal Parks of London*, 1978, pp. 32–3.

4 Frederick W. Trench, *Papers Relating to the Thames Quay; with Hints for Some Further Improvements in the Metropolis*, 1827

5 Deborah Jaffé, *Victoria: a Celebration of Queen and Empire*, 2000, pp. 34–5

6 Queen Victoria's Journal: 1 May 1851, quoted in Christopher Hibbert, *Queen Victoria in her Letters and Journals*, 2000, p. 84

7 The quotations in this paragraph are from William Andrews Nesfield, 'Architectural Gardens for Buckingham Palace 1849

submitted to HRH Prince Albert and the Commissioners for the Improvement of Buckingham Palace', Royal Institute of British Architects Drawings Collection.

8 Jane Brown, *The Art and Architecture of English Gardens: designs from the Collection of the Royal Institute of British Architects, 1609 to the Present Day*, 1989, pp. 80–81, 102–3

9 Queen Victoria to King Leopold of the Belgians, 24 February 1854, quoted in Hibbert, *Queen Victoria in her Letters and Journals*, p. 124

10 James Pope-Hennessy, *Queen Mary (1867–1953)*, 1959, p. 269

11 Pope-Hennessy, *Queen Mary*, p. 268

12 Queen Victoria's Journal: 6 July 1893, quoted in Hibbert, *Queen Victoria in her Letters and Journals*, p. 325

13 Frances Dimond, *Developing the Picture: Queen Alexandra and the Art of Photography*, forthcoming, October 2004

14 James Lees Milne, *The Enigmatic Edwardian: a Life of Reginald Brett, Lord Esher*, 1986, p. 134

15 Edna Healey, *The Queen's House: a Social History of Buckingham Palace*, 1997, p. 218

16 Queen Mary to Grand Duchess Augusta of Mecklenburg-Strelitz, 5 July 1914, in Pope-Hennessy, *Queen Mary*, p. 486

17 Queen Mary's Diary: 1 and 2 August 1914, in Pope-Hennessy, *Queen Mary*, p. 486

18 Queen Mary's Diary: 4 August 1914, in Pope-Hennessy, *Queen Mary*, p. 486

19 Photographs for 1914 are in Queen Mary's Photograph Album, vol. 17, covering the years 1913–16

20 Queen Mary's Diary: 11 November 1918, in Pope-Hennessy, *Queen Mary*, p. 509

21 Quoted by Elisa Segrave from her mother's diary, an exhibit in the Women and War exhibition, Imperial War Museum; *The Guardian*, G2, 15 October 2003

22 Julian Paget, *The Story of the Guards*, 1988, pp. 274–5

Chapter 4: The Gardeners' Garden

Opening quotation: David McClintock and Elinor Wiltshire, 'Wild and Naturalized Plants in Buckingham Palace Garden 1995–98', Supplement to *The London Naturalist*, no. 78, 1999, p. 28

1 *The Gardeners' Gazette*, ed. George Glenny, editorial, 14 October 1837

2 'The Royal Kitchen Gardens at Frogmore', in Jane Roberts, *Royal Landscape: the Gardens and Parks of Windsor*, 1997, pp. 241–5

3 Tom Fort, *The Grass is Greener: our Love Affair with the Lawn*, 2000, p. 125

4 RA PP/HH/985 Buckingham Palace Gardens Quarter to 30 June 1873

5 RA VIC/Q 18/87, Sir Thomas Biddulph to Queen Victoria, 1 July 1873

6 Philip Howard, *The Royal Palaces*, 1970, pp. 219–20

7   'The Gardens of England – Buckingham Palace', *The Garden*, 27 December 1873

8   V. Sackville-West immortalised this 'major prophet' in 'Gardens and Gardeners', *Country Notes*, 1939, pp. 96–108

9   David McClintock and Elinor Wiltshire, 'Wild and Naturalized Vascular Plants', Supplement to *The London Naturalist*, no. 78, 1999, p. 28

10 Fort, *The Grass is Greener*, pp. 145–6

11 Fort, *The Grass is Greener*, p. 147

12 L.A. Nickolls, *The Royal Story: a Diary of the Royal Year*, 1951, pp. 112–13

13 James Hogg and Michael Mortimer, eds., *The Queen Mother Remembered*, 2002, pp. 72–5

14 David L. Hawksworth, 'Lichens in Buckingham Palace Garden', Supplement to *The London Naturalist*, no. 78, 1999, p. 17

15 Fred Nutbeam (1914–1997), obituary in *The Times*, 7 June 1997

16 McClintock and Wiltshire, 'Wild and Naturalized Vascular Plants', Supplement to *The London Naturalist*, no. 78, 1999, p. 27

17 David McClintock, O.W. Richards and M. Knight, 'Natural History of the Garden of Buckingham Palace', *Proceedings and Transactions of the South London (Entomological & Natural History) Society*, 1964

18 Notably W.C. Teagle, *The Endless Village*, Nature Conservancy Council West Midlands Region, 1978; and see also Max Nicholson, *The Environmental Revolution*, Chapter 7, 'The British Story', 1970.

19 David Bellamy, *The Queen's Hidden Garden: Buckingham Palace's Treasury of Wild Plants*, with botanical paintings by Marjorie Lyon, 1984

20 Bellamy, *The Queen's Hidden Garden*, p. 173

21 David McClintock (1913–2001), obituary in *The Garden*, February 2002

22 David J. Carter, 'Butterflies and Moths etc.', Supplement to *The London Naturalist*, no. 80, 2001, pp. 169–91

23 S. Alex Williams, 'The Beetles of Buckingham Palace Garden', Supplement to *The London Naturalist*, no. 80, 2001, pp. 283–301

24 Alick Henrici, 'Non-lichenised Fungi in Buckingham Palace Garden', Supplement to *The London Naturalist*, no. 80, 2001, pp. 309–26

25 P.M. Greaves, 'The Tardigrade Fauna of Buckingham Palace Garden', Supplement to *The London Naturalist*, no. 80, 2001, pp. 111–13

26 Elinor Wiltshire, 'Bryophytes in Buckingham Palace Garden', Supplement to *The London Naturalist*, no. 78, 1999, pp. 23–6

27 Pryce Buckle, 'The Molluscan Fauna of Buckingham Palace Garden', Supplement to *The London Naturalist*, no. 78, 1999, pp. 81–6

28 Roy Sanderson, 'Birds in Buckingham Palace Garden', Supplement to *The London Naturalist*, no. 78, 1999, pp. 61–76

29 Clive Herbert, 'Mammals in Buckingham Palace Garden', Supplement to *The London Naturalist*, no. 78, 1999, pp. 77–9

30 Roy Sanderson, 'Birds in Buckingham Palace Garden', as n. 28 above

31 David McClintock and Mark Lane, 'Garden Plants', Supplement to *The London Naturalist*, no. 78, 1999, pp. 45–8

32 Olwen Hedley, *Queen Charlotte*, 1975, p. 85

33 The Wood & Ingram archive is a private collection but is currently being evaluated by Cambridgeshire Gardens Trust; see *Newsletter*, no. 14, May 2003 (CGT, The Grange, Easton, Huntingdon, Cambridgeshire PE18 0TU).

Chapter 5: Party Garden

Opening quotation: A.A. Milne, 'Buckingham Palace', *When We were Very Young*, 1924

1   Olwen Hedley, *Queen Charlotte*, 1975, p. 84

2   Hedley, *Queen Charlotte*, p. 82

3   *The London Magazine*, July 1762

4   *George Stubbs 1724–1806*, exh. cat., Tate Gallery/Yale Center for British Art/Salem House, 1984–5, p. 112, no. 77

5   Hedley, *Queen Charlotte*, p. 85

6   Wilfrid Blunt, *The Ark in the Park: the Zoo in the 19th Century*, 1976, p. 16

7   V.L. Kisling, ed., 'Estate Collections and the Windsor Great Park', *Zoo and Aquarium History: Ancient Animal Collections to Zoological Gardens*, 2001, pp. 56–8. See also 'Sandpit Gate and the Park Menageries', in Jane Roberts, *Royal Landscape: the Gardens and Parks of Windsor*, 1997, pp. 361–7.

8   Delia Millar, *Catalogue of the Victorian Watercolours in the Royal Collection*, 1995, Friedrich Wilhelm Keyl, p. 494, no. 3012

9   Millar, *Catalogue of the Victorian Watercolours*, Keyl, p. 494, no. 3016

10 Samuel Reynolds Hole, *Our Garden*, 1899, p. 3

11 Philip Magnus, *King Edward the Seventh*, 1967, pp. 519–20

12 Princess Alice, Duchess of Gloucester, *Memories of 90 Years*, 1991, pp. 14–15

13 Queen Victoria's Journal: 21 June 1887

14 Queen Victoria's Journal: 29 June 1887

15 RA LC/GEN/18/38, Margot Asquith (Countess of Oxford and Asquith) to Lord Clarendon, 16 July 1938. The couturier in question was Victor Stiebel.

16 RA MRH/GV/FUNC/242 (23 July 1931)

17 RA MRH/GV/FUNC/104/18. Constance Battersea to Sir Derek Keppel, 24 July 1925. Constance Battersea (born Rothschild) was a keen and romantic gardener as well as being a kindly philanthropist. See Jane Brown, *Lutyens and the Edwardians*, 1996, pp. 93–9.

LIST OF ILLUSTRATIONS

Reproductions of all items in the Royal Collection and all contemporary photographs of the garden by Christopher Simon Sykes © 2004 HM Queen Elizabeth II.

Royal Collection Enterprises are grateful for permission to reproduce the following:

Every effort has been made to contact copyright holders; any omissions are inadvertent, and will be corrected in future editions if notification of the amended credit is sent to the publisher in writing.

COMMEMORATIVE TREES

The happy custom of planting commemorative trees has helped to indicate their age and rate of growth. Although scattered around the garden, the majority are on or near the Round Bed at the end of the Conservatory Walk.

1. A copper beech (*Fagus sylvatica* Atropurpurea Group; BP 1875) on 15 March 1902, planted by King Edward VII and Queen Alexandra on the Main Lawn, shortly after he had ascended the throne. Although said 'not to be doing too well', it had reached 10m in 1963 and 17.5m in 1994.

2. A London plane (*Platanus x hispanica*; BP 4863), planted on the north front by King George V and Queen Mary on their twentieth wedding anniversary, 6 July 1913. 18.25m in 1994.

3. A London plane (*Platanus x hispanica*; BP 4887), planted for Princess Mary (later Princess Royal) on 15 October 1913 on the Round Bed. 13.7m in 1963, 16m in 1994 and 18m in 2000. This tree was for a long time labelled as *P. orientalis*; opinions vary.

4. A horse chestnut (*Aesculus hippocastanum*; BP 4968), planted by Prince Albert (later King Edward VIII) on 15 October 1914 in the Duke of Gloucester Recess. 11.8m in 1963, 16.2m in 1994 and 17.2m in 2001.

5. A horse chestnut (*Aesculus hippocastanum*; BP 1973), planted by Prince George (later Duke of Kent) on 13 April 1917 in the Duke of Kent Recess. 10.7m in 1963 and 18.2m in 1994.

6. A Caucasian lime (*Tilia x euchlora*; originally labelled *T. dasystyla*; BP 4851), planted for the Silver Wedding of King George V and Queen Mary in 1918 in the Guts. 13.1m in 1994 and 15m in 2000.

7. A Schwedler's Norway maple (*Acer platanoides* 'Schwedleri'; BP 4886), planted in March 1929 to replace a tree planted by the Prince of Wales in October 1913 on the Round Bed. 10.7m in 1963, 15.7m in 1994 and 16m in 2000.

8. An Indian horse chestnut (*Aesculus indica*; BP 4888), planted for Queen Mary on 2 December 1935 to commemorate the Silver Jubilee. 6.7m in 1963 and 14m in 1994.

9. An Indian horse chestnut (*Aesculus indica*; BP 4874), planted for King George V on 2 December 1935 to commemorate the Silver Jubilee. 7.6m in 1963 and 15.2m in 1994.

10. An Indian horse chestnut (*Aesculus indica*; BP 4891), planted for King George VI to commemorate the Coronation in 1937 [Coates 1978: 48]. 7.6m in 1963 and 16.1m in 1994.

11. An Indian horse chestnut (*Aesculus indica*; BP 4892), planted for Queen Elizabeth to commemorate the Coronation in 1937. 7.6m in 1963, 13.7m in 1994 and 15m in 2000.

12. An English oak (*Quercus robur*; BP 4893), planted by HRH Prince Charles on Good Friday 1954. The acorn from which this tree arose was germinated on 14 November 1948 to celebrate his birth. 3m in 1963 and 10.2m in 1994. It suffered from a severe attack of scale insects early in its life, which accounts for its much less vigorous habit in comparison with no. 13.

13. An English oak (*Quercus robur*; BP4894), planted for HRH Princess Anne on Good Friday 1954. The acorn from which this tree arose was germinated on 15 August 1950 to celebrate her birth. 9m in 1968 and 17.2m in 1994.

14. A double flowered cherry (*Prunus avium* 'Plena'; BP 1853), given by the Metropolitan Public Gardens Association for HRH Princess Anne and planted in 1957 on the Table area. 6.1m in 1963, 10.1m in 1994 and 11m in 2000.

15. A handkerchief tree (*Davidia involucrata* var. *vilmoriniana*), given by the Metropolitan Public Gardens Association for HRH Prince Charles and planted in 1957, originally on the Table area. Moved in 1964 to Clock Tree Corner. 11.7m in 1994.

16. An English oak (*Quercus robur*; BP 4844), from an acorn germinated at the time of the birth (19 February 1960) of HRH Prince Andrew, planted on 10 March 1969 in the centre of the garden. 7.9m in 1987 and 10.2m in 1994.

17. An English oak (*Quercus robur*; BP 4843), from an acorn germinated at the time of the birth (10 March 1964) of HRH Prince Edward, planted on 10 March 1969 in the Guts area of the garden. 6.1m in 1987 and 8.7m in 1994.

18. A cut-leaf beech (*Fagus sylvatica* var. *heterophylla* 'Aspleniifolia'; BP 1873), planted by HRH Prince Charles on his 21st birthday, 14 November 1969, on the Main Lawn. 10.2m in 1994.

19. A silver lime (*Tilia tomentosa*; BP 4862), planted by Lord Elworthy on the north front at the instance of the Royal Horticultural Society on the occasion of the Silver Jubilee of HM Queen Elizabeth II on 18 October 1977. 9m in 1994 and 13.1m in 2000.

20. A magnolia cultivar ('Elizabeth'), given to HM Queen Elizabeth II by Miss Elizabeth Scholtz of the Brooklyn Botanic Garden, New York. Planted in Aggies Recess in 1982.

21. A hybrid oak (*Quercus x libanerris* 'Rotterdam'; B 1191), presented by the Council of the International Dendrology Society after their visit on 23 October 1987. Planted by HM Queen Elizabeth II on 11 November 1989 on the Round Bed. 7.1m in 1998.

22. A rhododendron cultivar ('London Calling'), a new hybrid bred by Mark Lane at Buckingham Palace and presented to HM Queen Elizabeth II by the Royal Household Gardeners to celebrate her 70th birthday. It is in the area of the garden adjacent to Grosvenor Place (GP2), planted on 10 March 1997.

23. A hedge maple (*Acer campestre* 'Queen Elizabeth'), given to HM Queen Elizabeth II and HRH The Duke of Edinburgh by Queen Beatrix of The Netherlands to commemorate their Golden Wedding. Planted on 23 January 1998 at the Hyde Park Corner end of the garden. 5.1m in 1998.

24. A mulberry (*Morus latifolia* 'Spirata'; B 3489), given to HM Queen Elizabeth II and HRH The Duke of Edinburgh by the Metropolitan Public Gardens Association to commemorate their Golden Wedding. Planted on the Mound, facing the Palace, on 25 February 1998.

25. A yellow magnolia cultivar ('Butterflies'; 2002/0086), given to HM Queen Elizabeth II by the Metropolitan Parks and Gardens Association to celebrate the Golden Jubilee. Planted on 16 April 2002 in the King's Border.

The 'BP' and 'B' and other numbers assigned to plants in the garden at Buckingham Palace are part of an ongoing exercise to identify as many plants in the garden as possible. The 'BP' numbers were the first to be assigned, as part of the survey of the garden in the 1990s. The numbers are now generated by and recorded on a computer database.

ACKNOWLEDGEMENTS

Writing the history of 'this favourite spot of Ground' has been a pleasure and a privilege: I am indebted to Her Majesty The Queen for Gracious Permission to undertake this study and make use of material in the Royal Archives, and to His Royal Highness The Duke of Edinburgh for the Foreword.

An idea for a book on the garden at Buckingham Palace was originally mooted by the naturalist and heather expert the late David McClintock, and I should like to acknowledge the generosity of his executors Andrew and Hugh McClintock in allowing me to use their father's papers.

I should also like to thank Christopher Simon Sykes for undertaking the photography for this book.

At Windsor Castle I was welcomed by the Librarian, Jane Roberts, and I am grateful for her continued support and advice – along with that of Frances Dimond, Curator of the Royal Photograph Collection; and Pamela Clark, Jill Kelsey, Allison Derrett and the staff of the Royal Archives. I should also like to offer my thanks to Shruti Patel and Karen Lawson, and to Bridget Wright, Susan Owens and Margaret Westwood of the Royal Library and Print Room at Windsor.

At Buckingham Palace I received kind and courteous help, for which I thank Gill Middleburgh, Anita Wilson, Emily Powell, Stuart Neil, Alex Garty of Royalty Protection, and the Property Manager, Roy Brown, and Isabelle Brotherton-Ratcliffe and the staff of the Master of the Household's department. I am particularly grateful to Mark Lane, Head Gardener at Buckingham Palace whilst I was researching and writing, for his generosity with his time and his unrivalled knowledge of the garden. He is now Gardens Manager for the royal gardens in London and at Windsor and Daniel Cairns has succeeded him at Buckingham Palace.

My thanks go additionally to Jacky Colliss Harvey, Frances Dunkels and Jonathan Marsden at the Royal Collection in London. For help with specific queries I should like to thank Rachel, Lady Coventry, Jill Cremer and John Drake. Christine Groom has interpreted my original typescript with her usual skill, which is much appreciated. As always with my books I am indebted to the ever-helpful staff at The London Library and at Cambridge University Library, and especially in this instance to the National Archives at Kew, the Royal Horticultural Society Lindley Library and the Cambridge Botanic Garden library. The published sources for the story of Buckingham Palace garden are very varied and I should like to express my appreciation for all of these, which I have made every endeavour to acknowledge adequately in the notes, while some of the more recent and more relevant books are mentioned in the Introduction.

For their cheerful efficiency in dealing with my text and in responding to my requests for elusive illustrations my thanks go to Rosamonde Williams, Karen Weaver, Jenny Knight, Liz Heasman, Debbie Wayment, Bev Zimmern, Marcus Fletcher and Alison Worthington at Book Production Consultants; my special appreciation to Karen Stafford, the book's designer.

While I was working on this book I heard BBC Radio Four's programme in tribute to the broadcaster Harold Williamson, known for his candid interviews with children; in one of the most famous he was reliably informed by a 7-year-old interviewee that 'The Queen wore her crown when she walked out in her garden'. This has not been a book of 'royal revelations' so far, but perhaps I may close with one – that, to the very best of my knowledge, Her Majesty does not!

Jane Brown
Elton, May 2004

INDEX